Revised & Expanded Edition

SIFE, WALLACE

THE LOSS OF A PET

THREE WEEKS

"Old Drum Memorial." The bronze plaque beneath the statue contains the entire text of a speech by the late Senator Vest of Missouri. In the 1870 trial of a man from Warrensburg, who had wantonly shot a neighbor's dog, Vest asked $200 in damages. After this brief but effective speech, the jury deliberated only two minutes and awarded the plaintiff $500.   *Courtesy, City of Warrensburg, MO*

Revised & Expanded Edition

The Loss of a Pet

WALLACE SIFE, PH.D.

HOWELL
BOOK
HOUSE

New York

MACMILLAN is a registered trademark of Macmillan, Inc.

Howell Book House
A Simon & Schuster Macmillan Company
1633 Broadway
New York, NY 10019

Macmillan Publishing books may be purchased for business or sales promotional use. For information please write: Special Markets Department, Macmillan Publishing USA, 1633 Broadway, New York, NY 10019.

Library of Congress Cataloging-in-Publication Data
Sife, Wallace.
    The loss of a pet / Wallace Sife. --New rev. ed.
        p.   cm.
    Includes index.
    ISBN 0-87605-197-2
    1. Pet owners--Psychology.   2. Pets--Death--Psychological aspects.
3. Bereavement--Psychological aspects.   I. Title
SF411.47.S54   1998
155.9'37--dc21   97-41254
                                                          CIP

Manufactured in the United States of America
10   9   8   7   6   5   4

Book design by Scott Meola
Cover Design by Kevin Hanek

To peace and permanence, in the loving memory of my pal,
Dachshund Edel Meister, MS, CD (1979–1987),
and all his soul mates who were beloved,
and the good people who mourn our common loss.

TRIBUTE TO THE DOG

The following speech was made by the late Senator Vest of Missouri in the trial of a man at Warrensburg, who had wantonly shot a dog belonging to a neighbor. Mr. Vest represented the plaintiff, who demanded $200 in damages. As a result of this speech, the jury, after two minutes of deliberation, awarded the plaintiff $500.

"Gentlemen of the jury: The best friend a man has in this world may turn against him and become his enemy. His son or daughter that he has reared with loving care may prove ungrateful. Those who are nearest and dearest to us, those whom we trust with our happiness and our good name, may become traitors to their faith. The money that a man has, he may lose. It flies away from him, perhaps when he needs it the most. A man's reputation may be sacrificed in a moment of ill considered action. The people who are prone to fall on their knees to do us honor when success is with us may be the first to throw the stone of malice when failure settles its cloud upon our heads. The one absolutely unselfish friend that a man can have in this selfish world, the one that never deserts him and the one that never proves ungrateful or treacherous is his dog.

"Gentlemen of the jury, a man's dog stands by him in prosperity and in poverty, in health and in sickness. He will sleep on the cold ground, where the wintry winds blow and the snow drives fiercely, if only he may be near his master's side. He will kiss the hand that has no food to offer, he will lick the wounds and sores that come in encounters with the roughness of the world. He guards the sleep of his pauper master as if he were a prince. When all other friends desert he remains. When riches take wings and reputation falls to pieces, he is as constant in his love as the sun in its journey through the heavens. If fortune drives the master forth an outcast in the world, friendless and homeless, the faithful dog asks no higher privilege than that of accompanying him to guard against danger, to fight against his nemies, and when the last scene of all comes, and death takes the master in its embrace and his body is laid away in the cold ground, no matter if all other friends pursue their way, there by his grave side will the noble dog be found, his head between his paws, his eyes sad but open in alert watchfulness, faithful and true even to death."

Courtesy of The Daily Star-Journal Warrensburg, MO
Inscribed on the Old Drum Memorial Warrensburg, MO 1870

CONTENTS

INTRODUCTION

Grief must have a purpose,
otherwise it is meaningless and destructive.

*I*f you are the very special kind of person who grieves deeply for
the loss of a beloved pet, this book is written for you. Or, if you
have a pet now and love it dearly, these pages can help enhance
your awareness and joy in its companionship. Unfortunately, all living things die, and although you can never be really prepared for that,
what is offered here can help you draw upon your love to minimize
your grief and pain when death eventually does happen. Although
this may seem maudlin, it really is an important part of your celebration of the joyous life and very special love you had together.

What is presented in these pages will help you realize that you are
not alone. Many others have suffered the same anguish, and what we
have learned about this tragic experience can help you. This book
will explain this exceptionally painful and mystifying impact on your
life and show how you can manage it. The shock of loss and bereavement is one of the most profound emotional traumas we can experience and should be nothing to feel ashamed about.

It is important to know that the exceptional feelings and irrational
periods we go through at this time are a common symptom of intense
mourning. Since so little has been known about pet bereavement up
until recently, it is natural to wonder whether such powerful reactions
for a pet are normal. Because of this lack of information, many rational people question their own sanity at such nerve-wracking
moments. What you will learn about yourself and your bereavement
will convince you that you are not in any way losing your mind. The
loss of a pet is a unique shock, and the pain and confusion you are
experiencing will be demystified. This knowledge will help you with
your grief and distress.

There is no easy answer to how long the deep grief of mourning
will last. It helps the healing process when we change or modify our
daily routines that formerly involved the deceased pet. Often, too
many constant physical reminders and associations left about the

house become very upsetting. It would be useful to remove or monitor some of these, for the time being at least. If we allow ourselves to speak about our loss and grieve freely, the mourning period will be shorter and more constructive. We let some of the pain out this way, which makes room for healing. Indeed, in clinical studies it has been found that some people have never truly completed their mourning needs and process. Therefore, they suffer more than they should and bear their grief needlessly for many years—even for the rest of their lives.

Human beings are creatures of habit and structure. We find security in routines and established orders. Our individual personalities form powerful subconscious templates for our behaviors. Living with a beloved pet for an extended part of our lives produces new patterns that become permanent. All of us lovingly adapt our lifestyles around this cherished adopted family member. We become completely conditioned to the routines. This habituated way of life with a beloved pet is taken for granted, and we go on as if it will never end. But it does, and suddenly it is gone! We can never be really prepared for this, and the resultant shock is normal. Our whole life goes through a violent emotional upheaval. It is as if a great jagged hole had been ripped out of one's life.

One cannot avoid contact with persons who say that we should not suffer real bereavement for a pet, which is a mere animal who can easily be replaced. Such ignorant responses reflect *their* personal problems and should not become ours, especially at this very painful and vulnerable time of loss. Without exception, these cynical critics have never known the unique love of a pet, proving themselves unqualified to judge us in this grief. They are not pet-oriented people. But be grateful for any sincere attempts by others, however awkward, to ease your pain. You must learn to make this important distinction.

In our hour of need it can at first seem that there are not many people who can comprehend our bereavement. As a defensive posture we learn to readjust our relationships with others, including close family members. This can be extremely disappointing or even aggravating at times. We must also learn to be cautious and avoid hasty angry over-reactions, which are more easily experienced now, but which may later be regretted. Our sense of justified anger too often can override our common sense, during this especially unstable time of our life. We are most vulnerable at this point of crisis and confusion, and we have to keep all of our best interests in mind.

For many valid reasons, the mourning for a pet can be far more intense than for a human. This will be explained in more detail in a later chapter. The pain you are experiencing now is real, and in many ways, it is very debilitating. You are actually mourning the death of your dearest friend, as well as a very close member of your immediate family, nothing less!

Death, in general, is a subject that most people in Western cultures are very uncomfortable with. Discussion of the subject is awkward or even impossible. People don't know how to handle it without embarrassment, evasion or pretense. They use euphemisms, which attempt to provide evasive expressions for more specific terms and ideas. You may discover that the passing of your cherished companion pet is too difficult or distressing to discuss with people who are not completely sympathetic with your loss. You probably also have experienced situations in which you were forced to feel defensive and secretive about your bereavement.

Historically, Western tradition and religion have avoided the subject of pet death, leaving the full responsibility and burden solely up to the confused, lonely and distraught mourner of a beloved animal. Up until very recently each person had to suffer alone. Now we have become an acknowledged community within our ever-changing society, and our bereavement needs are being met—in greater degrees every year.

Individual pastoral counseling in this context, if it can be found, may offer some help. But the death of animals is not officially acknowledged by most of the world's major religions. There are many who believe the concept of a soul includes any sentient being that is endowed with love. But this is too often met with skepticism and doubt. Only in the past few years has some theological adjustment been made to address the problems of pet death and bereavement. It is expected that in the future, official doctrines will adapt to these more contemporary needs. This book presents an unusual chapter, partly composed of brief articles by some religious leaders, which attempts to address the rising problem of the death of pets. The spiritual needs and considerations of modern society are changing with our socio-economic evolution.

Pets have become more significant, loved members of most households. Aside from veterinary care, a $20 billion annual business now caters to the needs and care of pets in the United States alone. All this economic pressure has its influence on us, through advertising, products on the shelves, new jobs in the industry and a thousand other ways that affect us in our normal daily lives. Today, you see more pets than ever on television and in the movies. And they're showing up in greater frequency in literature and even songs. Why is this happening? America loves pets, and our changing lifestyles are making us better able to appreciate this. We are a nation of pets, and the grief suffered in their loss is a subject that is becoming much better understood, respected and accepted.

It is amazing how often we hear of people who are in deep grief over the death of a beloved pet. Unfortunately, their plight had customarily been put aside as something unusual. But since this is a human story now being heard so often, we should be getting a strong message from it. There are huge numbers of all kinds of pets in the United States alone. Aside from birds and other rarer kinds of animals, today there are over 110 million pet dogs and cats who are continually reproducing and dying. Literally, millions of people every year are affected by the death of a family pet, and they are all hurting, in varying degrees. Because of the enormous numbers of people involved so emotionally, bereavement for a beloved pet is becoming more accepted as a normal social experience. Now it is also much easier to find a support group of others who know from experience what you are going through.

Dynamic changes in contemporary civilization are causing the disappearance of the extended household and a decrease in family size. Along with a very rapidly growing population, there are now more single, divorced and widowed people than ever before. This particular element of our social structure owns more pets than most others. Lonely people, in particular, are well aware of the wonderful love and therapeutic effects companion animals have in enriching their lives.

In many ways, the beloved pet becomes a symbol of our own secret selves. It represents an innocence and grace we feel but cannot express to other humans. Without a pet, this important self-discovery may never be made. This is only one more reason, out of many, for the intensity of grief and bereavement for such a death. It feels as if the best part of our self has died with the pet, and we weep for that as well. Another thing that affects us is that the pet is a loving soul, and we mourn it accordingly. We want to believe that it has gone to some other realm and that someday we will be there, to join again. Although nobody really knows the answer, too little is ever spoken of this, leaving us even more upset during our especially vulnerable time of need.

Who has not experienced that special sense of excitement and greeting when we put the key in the lock and open the door? To our pet, just coming home was a major event. Over the years we had become so used to anticipating our pet's welcome, from a meow to a tail-thumping salute. Now the home is shockingly silent and feels empty. But the pet's presence still seems to be everywhere. At this early stage, it is normal to imagine for a fleeting second that we hear special sounds made by our pet. After this loss we still live in the echoes of the loving patterns that became our way of life.

The loss of a pet also has another meaning for some. There are many heartbroken people who have literally lost their pets. Whether this was caused by their wandering off, unexpected happenings or circumstances, or even theft, the loving pet owners are thrown into a special crisis not comparable to anything else. Among other anxieties, they grieve and worry whether their pet will be sold to an experimental lab, or if it will be injured or killed by cars or other animals. It could also end up unidentified in a pound somewhere, where it would be euthanized, along with the millions of other poor strays in this country each year. This is an especially horrible kind of loss, where there rarely is a happy ending. These loving pet owners are also in a state of mourning and will go through all the painful stages of bereavement you will learn about later, especially unresolved guilt. A special chapter on this unique loss has been added for their benefit.

Often during pet bereavement, the people we rely on most fall short of our needs and expectations. At times, we are fortunate to find a caring, supportive new friend, usually another pet owner, who can share our unique feelings and responses. Such understanding is wonderful, but too rare. Up until now there have been far too few things published in any of the mass media on this subject. But all that is changing.

A few years ago my own dog, Edel Meister, died very unexpectedly. Despite my special training in human bereavement, my grief was intense and inconsolable. I was desolate for at least two weeks before

I could make even a weak pretense at functioning normally again. Pet bereavement was little understood or respected then, except in a few small, isolated circles. I had to painfully crawl my way through my own intense grief and debility to get to a perspective on what this is all about. After much time and research, armed with this new knowledge, I resolved to write the book that was sorely needed by others. It is dedicated as a loving, living testament to Edel Meister's cherished memory—and to all the other beloved pets in this world throughout history. This is the best memorial I can give him.

I hope this book will give you what you need to help yourself through the agonizing parts of your mourning. It is offered with affection and care in the hope that your loved one inspires you to live on through the pain and grow, as mine did

Wallace Sife, Ph.D.
Brooklyn, New York

CHAPTER I

The Human-Pet Bond

Everything that lives, lives not alone nor for itself.

—William Blake

T he human-pet bond is one that dates back to prehistoric times. Some cave drawings depict dogs joining in the hunt, as well as dogs in the camp and around the fire, sharing the lives of our earliest ancestors. That initial bond was not an accident or rare occurrence, but rather a natural, deliberate interaction. It served both the basic needs of humans and these friendly cousins of the wolves. These needs included mutual protection and companionship, in addition to improved hunting. Much later, dogs would be trained and specially bred for herding and other purposes.

THE DOMESTICATION OF ANIMALS

Early dogs were valued as friendly hunting adjuncts and reliable alarms, warning of intruders. Since human survival was a hand-to-mouth daily challenge, the dogs were left to fend for themselves, but were occasionally thrown bones and scraps of food (even as they are today in certain undeveloped countries). Much later, during biblical times, pets as we consider them now were still nowhere to be found, aside from an occasionally favored livestock animal. Once in a while,

"Faithful and Constant
Companions."
*Courtesy, Hartsdale Canine
Cemetery, Inc.*

In memory of a precious cat.

Courtesy, Abbey Glen Pet Memorial Park

a family would take an adorable lamb or kid into the house and bring it up by hand, allowing the children to play with it. In those hard times, this practice had to be temporary. Animals were primarily raised for meat and milk, and most of the favored ones were eventually slaughtered. Times were much tougher then, and food on the plate was a family's first concern. Shelter, reproduction and just staying alive were always primary, and anything else had much lower priority in each day's survival. This pet-keeping was still so occasional that there was not even a word to define it. The times were not yet ready for our present-day concept of a non-utility companion animal. Favored household animals were temporary indulgences— extravagances that generally did not fit into the normal long-term scheme of harsh, daily existence at that time.

Cats were revered in ancient Egypt as quasi-religious figures, and they were killed and mummified as part of a rite we still do not fully understand. But they were natural predators, and survived and increased, independently, especially well around farms and granaries, where they were welcomed and appreciated. Cats served a vital need in the growing agrarian development of our civilization. The rats and mice they hunted were hated for devouring precious grain and other foods. This was particularly apparent when there was a scant supply for people to eat. Much later, cats became even more valued when rats and mice were also found to spread disease.

Documentation shows that the actual word "pet" first came into use in the Old Northern English and Scottish languages only about to any favored animal who was domesticated (or tamed) and treated with indulgence or fondness. This practice had become much more common by then. Our modern concept of a household pet dog or cat was just beginning its evolution with this first coining of the word.

Nature has prescribed that very few animals can be domesticated, and even fewer can be tamed. When early man began to emerge from the cave, he learned to take advantage of all the animals that could possibly be cultivated for food. Throughout the millennia, people selectively bred the many lines of livestock animals that have become so familiar today. But as civilizations eventually grew, dogs and cats, through their normal affectionate behavior, gradually insinuated themselves into the homes and families of humans. Actually, the attraction was mutual and unavoidable. Since the social natures of cats and dogs are so different from all other animals, it was only natural that they adopted themselves into our lives—and something deep within our human nature loved it. The transition that occurred was dramatic when the favored domesticated farm animal became the tame but free-ranging dog or cat who lived with us. This helped set the stage for our modern concept of family pets. We were only just beginning to discover the wonders of the human-pet bond.

When early civilizations developed, rich men and nobles were the only people who could afford any luxuries. They enjoyed slaves, fine foods, clothes, jewels and all the indulgences that most people could only dream of. Dogs were selectively bred to serve specialized hunting functions or to display certain aesthetic appearances. Possessing these dogs became a matter of pride to their wealthy owners. Because of the inherent affectionate nature of humans, however, it was impossible for man and dog or cat to live under the same roof and not form a loving bond. As civilizations advanced, the keeping of pet animals gradually became an established practice. The only exceptions to this are found in extremely fundamental religious societies. It is interesting to note that even today these groups still do not have a vocabulary word for a pet. Strict traditionalists will not assimilate this relatively new practice into their lives because there were no biblical or other scriptural references to pets.

By the middle of the eighteenth century, more and more people began keeping pet dogs and cats for amusement, entertainment and eventually companionship. It is important to realize that this was only about 250 years ago. It did not take long for us to discover the very rich source of love that these companion animals provide. Once we were able to afford the luxury of bonding to a pet, we were never the same. At this time in our history the number of household pets began to increase very rapidly. Sailors started bringing home tame monkeys and talking parrots from exotic places, but the rest of us were beginning to discover the unique loving companionship of dogs and cats.

PETS FILL OUR NEED TO LOVE AND NURTURE

Humans have a basic and fundamental need to give love and to nurture. This is best demonstrated by the innate tendency that children have to lovingly care for their dolls and toy animals. Even some adults still enjoy the pleasure of owning such toys. The inherent love of soft, cuddly and furry things can be seen in the behavior of the human baby. Dolls and toy animals are made into fantasy pals and treated with great personal care and affection. As we grow up, this loving human instinct is usually transferred to more traditional objects of affection. We do not outgrow the natural tendency for stroking small animals and taking care of dolls as though they are babies. It offers a sense of personal reassurance to many people.

The need to nurture is part of our innate makeup that helps to ensure the preservation of our species. In evolutionary terms, this is an essential instinct that grew as a result of the drive for survival. It is a basic part of our very nature, and it carries over to our beloved companion animals. Pets are the perfect solution for our need to nurture and love when we are not too involved in the rearing of our own babies. Soon enough though, the companion animal becomes an unmatched companion for the young child, as well as the harried parent. It would seem as if nature had put certain animals on this earth to share their lives with us. Pets have become a basic part of our social evolution. A natural and symbiotic relationship has developed, greatly benefiting our mutual emotional and survival needs. Without pets our lives would be far less productive and a lot lonelier.

The pleasures derived from keeping a companion animal go beyond any objective comments that can be listed here. They give us innocent dependence, companionship and love. Above all, a pet is totally accepting and is never judgmental. With time, the unique emotional bonding between the pet and the owner intensifies for each. The result is a wonderful coupling that gives us added stability, purpose and a sense of personal enrichment that defies description.

The bond we develop with pets is as wonderful and rewarding as it is fascinating and practical. It is an active reaching out and sharing of life with another living being, who happens not to be human. This relationship offers us a chance to share and express our pure selves, without needing to defend our actions or feelings. Companion animals, as we have come to call them, give us our greatest opportunities to express love, without ever having to worry about being judged or rejected. They give us back a devotion that is unmatched by any other relationship, in a very private bond. Pets provide us with an oasis of unqualified love and acceptance in an otherwise demanding and critical world. Their obedience and respect give us an increased sense of self-worth that adds new meaning to our lives. In return, we assimilate them into positions of great personal value.

Some are so innocent and transparent in their needs and feelings that we get to know and trust them better than most humans. And the pets probably feel the same about us. We touch and caress them freely and speak to them adoringly. And they respond with love and many different kinds of reassurances we need. Stroking is very enriching emotionally, , however, but it is an expression of feeling that is still highly guarded in most other social expressions. The pleasure of petting a companion animal has been proven to be of significant medical and psychological benefit, as well: Blood pressure is reduced, heartbeat is improved, resistance to disease is heightened and tension is eased, among other tangible benefits. All this just from stroking our pets! This relationship has a dimension that transcends even the ties between people, as wonderful as they can be.

We open up completely to pets, and we receive an inner sense of joy and strength at the adoration we receive in return. It has often been noted that pets can be truer friends than people. Because they are never critical, and therefore allow us to blossom emotionally in ways that would not be possible with fellow humans, who tend to be competitive and judgmental. We make our pets our secret sharers, allowing them greater trust than what is often given to friends, families or even spouses.

Sometimes these expressions of our very private selves are taken out of proportion to what is safe or normal. There are pet lovers who have forsaken some or much of their inter-human relationships for the sense of love and security their pets give them. They can isolate themselves with their pets from the rest of the world which may seem too threatening, painful or dangerous. That can prove very unhealthy in the long run. There are many people who live lives of quiet desperation and who become too dependent on a pet for supportiveness in stressful social situations. Frequently, when there is a strong conflict between two family members, one of them will turn to the pet for comfort and love and for the sense of supportiveness he or she needs. This dependent relationship becomes very personal and secret. With time, it grows in magnitude and can distort things if the discord is not resolved.

LEARNING TO BE RESPONSIBLE TO OURSELVES

It is a wonderful experience to love and care for a pet. However, we must love ourselves as well in order to survive and continue to lead productive lives. We must not lose awareness of our being part of a larger social structure. Aside from civic responsibility, we have a humane responsibility to ourselves. We need to grow and prosper and find our place within the community of humans. Lonely people who despair of finding love and being needed often turn to pets. That is all well and good, but it should not become an escape or substitute, or offer an emotional buffer that isolates them from human companionship. With the inevitable death of the pet, this personal oasis evaporates. We too easily set ourselves up to be very vulnerable to the loneliness, grief and bereavement that comes when we lose a pet.

Man is basically an emotional animal, and we must love and feel important to keep our balance. The special challenges of living in an increasingly fast-paced, impersonal society compound our problems. Despite this, our needs must be filled regardless of how we do it. We need to find an outlet or substitute to serve this, and we seek it in another person, a pet, a hobby or even our work. Too often, we do not have someone very dear to love or fully trust, and we are driven elsewhere to satisfy this need as best we can. There are also those who excessively immerse themselves in their work or hobbies to sublimate a similar basic need for ego reinforcement, or to keep from feeling lonely. A large percentage of today's city dwellers is composed of people living alone with their beloved companion animals.

Insecurity often drives even the best of us, and some may feel that the only love and respect we can get is from a pet. Forced by low self-esteem or personal vulnerability, many people tend to become overly dependent on this sure relationship, within an otherwise uncaring, ever-threatening society. Personal happiness is often measured by the safe life and uncompromised bond we share with pets. Many people feel isolated from the rest of the world—secure with this love within a very private, emotional cocoon. Unfortunately, when these in-timate companions die, that security is breached. The profound shock of being bereft in this manner can seem unbearable. We are catapulted into a state of shock that cannot be easily compared to anything else.

A great many people find that their love for and from companion animals becomes the saving grace in their lives. To anyone who has ever had a dear pet, this makes great sense. Certainly, there is nothing wrong with adoring a faithful companion animal, despite what some bitter, self-proclaimed critics would say. People who are not pet lovers cannot really understand this special bond. Pets give absolute love to their masters, regardless of how disapproved of or ignored they may be by the rest of the world. The lowliest and most downtrodden person is always lord and master to his adoring pet. The unique bond that is established becomes an empowering and enriching experience. This has always been understood by the privileged few. But now we have become many, and the others who still don't understand the owner-pet relationship are becoming less critical and more open and curious.

Today, a darling companion animal is considered a normal part of one's immediate family. In the case of a person who lives alone with a pet, the mutual bonding becomes a complex and intimate relationship. However, death is the one thing we cannot protect a pet from, and it is the one subject in life that we least understand. It scares most of us to extremes of avoidance in Western society; we almost never contemplate or discuss it. We continually attempt to disregard the unavoidable. When death inevitably catches up with our pets, we are almost always shocked and unprepared. We are also often filled with irrational feelings of guilt because we couldn't delay or prevent its death.

Our culture encourages avoidance in dealing with the discussion, philosophy and ultimate reality of death. The subject is considered so disagreeable that many people feel it is impolite to even mention the word, and choose to use euphemisms instead. Death is perceived to be bad, the ultimate enemy, and much too scary to confront directly. So we only allude to it indirectly, when we are finally forced to face it. Many people are glad to leave the details to the professional thanatologists and clergy and relieve themselves of fearful and unknown responsibilities and reactions. But this avoidance leaves us very vulnerable.

In many ways, a pet is very similar to a totally beloved and dependent child who never grows up. In such a relationship, our sense of bonding and responsibility becomes very profound and complicated.

One's secret self is intimately involved in such a relationship deep within the subconscious. In this modern world of rushing about and perceiving things through sound bites and superficialities, many people feel safer confiding their most sensitive feelings only to an adoring companion animal. It is absolutely accepting and faithful to us, and it will never fail our love and trust—except to die.

When sensitive individuals lose a pet, their bereavement is often very different than for a human. It may at first seem remarkable, but many normal people can grieve more for a dear pet than for a close relative or friend—or sometimes even a spouse. Mourning for a pet is usually not comparable to any other kind of mourning. We share a large part of our lives with pets, including intimate feelings we could never trust or communicate to another person.

The relationships we develop with our pets define the quality and style of our lives. They are what we make them, and we ultimately become products of this relationship. We can love them as pets, as surrogate children or as replacements for other people. We can dote on them, squandering our precious energies and time, or we can treat them as joyful companions in our own trek through life. That is our individual choice.

As we see, the bond between humans and pets has changed dramatically, from biblical through modern times. Today, they are only rarely used as working animals, as in herding or hunting. At this time, a desire for the special company of a pet is all the justification we need. The most important function that animal companionship now serves is a psychological one. The pet's presence is comforting and full of love, restoring and reinforcing the ego strength and self-image of its master. Thus, the evolving human-pet bond has become a modern phenomenon in an increasingly mechanical world.

ACCEPTING THE LOSS

In our society, males have a much more difficult time during the bereavement period. They have been conditioned by a lifetime of restrictive customs and cultural mores, and disciplined that it is not manly to cry, even in private. Fortunately, we are gaining insight into this controlling of behavior. Sexual stereotyping is something we are starting to do something about. Ours is an age of beginning enlightenment on many levels, as never before in history.

With the human-pet bond growing so pervasive and strong in recent times, we have come to a changing point in human behavior. Pet bereavement and its related problems are emerging as a new social phenomenon of our Western culture. The growing visibility of vast pet-related industries is also causing a new public awareness of some of the ramifications of this once little-understood bond.

The sharing between people and pets offers many private and precious moments together. They are as unique as they are intensely personal and gratifying. Such mutual love is its own greatest justification for us to ever find joy in our pets, as well as ourselves. Children have their security blankets; we have our pets.

We get much love and delight from them in life, and we grieve deeply for them when they die. Because of the unique enhancement they give to our lives, they become a treasured part of us forever. When a pet's life ends, more dies than just a beloved companion animal. Since we make them into living symbols of our own innocence and purest feelings, a treasured secret part of each of us also dies. This can be reborn as we slowly pick up our shattered emotional pieces and move on. At this point in our healing, it is often natural to feel a need for a spiritual reunion with the pet. It is in our nature to want to believe that our souls will meet again, and in a better way when we eventually follow them. This feeling stays with us for the rest of our lives, in living tribute to our bond.

Responsibility

He prayeth well who loveth well both man and bird and beast.

—*Samuel Taylor Coleridge*

When we make that wonderful decision to have a pet, we create an amazing spectrum of responsibilities for ourselves. It is similar to the obligations of caring for a child. In some ways, caring for a pet is even more difficult, since children grow up, become independent and outlive us. Pets do not. They are bound to us for everything, all of their lives. When they die, the responsibilities we created change, yet live on in many new ways. Our obligations shift to providing greater care and consideration to ourselves, and the concerned people in our lives who seem unable to grasp the full extent of our plight. We owe them something, also.

The initial decision to have a pet comes with an acceptance of a burden of total obligation and reliability. This includes caring for every possible aspect of the pet's life; the health, happiness and well-being. We volunteer for a duty that quickly becomes a passion, an act of love. As our pets become more and more endeared to us, this responsibility becomes a routine, rearranging basic patterns in our lives. We bond to them permanently, and care and provide for them as we would with dependent children. In a very real sense, they become a part of us.

CARE PROVIDERS

As self-appointed stewards, we are totally and singly responsible for the pet's life and well-being. In a sense, we assume godlike roles to them. They look to us to provide and care for *everything* they experience. But despite our desire to arrange and care, we cannot control the universe. We are unable to protect them from all possible dangers. Accidents and illnesses will happen. When bad things happen, the pet owner can fall victim to what feels like failed responsibility, with all its invented reactions of guilt. Our wisdom sometimes becomes clouded by our human frailty. There are moments when our duty is defined by a complexity of circumstances that can be truly beyond our control or comprehension, at the time.

We must provide everything for the pet and assume a responsibility that cannot be taken casually. We must deal with nutrition, medical care, toys, playmates, status and quality of life—as well as anything else that may be of concern. Also, there are daily feedings; the water dish has to be checked regularly; visual checkups on the pet's appearance and health must be made constantly; and the long list goes on. Strangely enough, the practice of this constant total care strengthens our bond with our pets. We invest time and attention and become even more responsible and loving. This personal investment has its rewards, too. It admits us into a private world of mutual love and pleasure with our pets. But oddly enough, that can have its bad sides, too.

This mutual bonding becomes a wonderful exchange of need and fulfillment between owner and pet. We involve our dear animal friends in a unique relationship that shares a much more personal side of us than we safely entrust to any human. Because of a pet's innocent and complete dependency on us, we sometimes lose perspective in expressing our overall sense of responsibility.

COPING WITH DEATH

In an ironic psychological turnabout, we can become too dependent on our pets and rely too heavily on their needing us. There is no place for death in our loving scheme of things. In our society, the discussion or consideration of death has been taboo. We know next to nothing about death, and any associations regarding it are very upsetting at best. It scares and mystifies us. Therefore, we discreetly avoid its examination or even the briefest reference to it, whenever we can. When the pet eventually dies, as all must, the shock can easily be distorted into a subconscious sense of intense personal failure. As ready as we are intellectually, we are never really prepared emotionally for the death of a pet. We all need as much help as we can get. At this time, we need to draw on our own inner resources. But at such an emotional time, this insight is not available to us.

Very often, even our closest friends and family can't grasp the depth and extent of our bereavement. Often, we suffer with a sense of guilt and failed responsibility. Justified or not, these feelings become an extremely private and personal matter that we need to hide from the rest of the world. Others close to us may seem to fail us at this time as well, because of their lack of understanding or acceptance of our self-made role. If they are not pet lovers, or if they have a fear of the subject of death, their inability to respond in more supportive ways may be intensified. We owe it to them, as well as to ourselves, not to be hair-triggered; it is important to try to maintain some degree of control during these difficult times. There are exceptions to this, however, and personal relationships often change when one is grieving for a pet.

As suggested earlier, when a beloved pet dies we lose a very close member of our immediate family. We lose a treasured extension of ourselves. But the responsibility we have taken on is not yet finished; we must live on without the pet. That obligation to ourselves is one that we have to honor during this especially difficult period of grief. Healing our pain is a responsibility we owe to ourselves. If our loving companion animals could speak to us from beyond the grave, that is exactly what they would ask us to do. When enduring the loss of a pet, we must either prepare for the experience in advance or, in healthy hindsight, open ourselves to a new awareness. That is where expert bereavement counseling and books like this can be of enormous help.

Aside from mortuary care and expense, our obligation to the pet lives on. Now we must make its memory a positive, treasured part of ourselves, never to be lost. Too many mourners allow themselves to fall apart, losing all signs of personal control. This is not necessarily a bad reaction. But admittedly, we really don't know how to respond to

Monument to a gallant soldier.
Photo by George Wirt,
© Bide-A-Wee 1992

SARGE
SERIAL 806   TATTOO Z810
BELGIAN SHEPHERD
SERVED AS SCOUT
U.S. ARMY
WITH 34TH DIVISION
ITALIAN CAMPAIGN
WORLD WAR II
1943–1946
MADE LANDINGS AT
ANZIO BEACHHEAD
AND SALERNO
SAVED MANY LIVES
BY HIS ABILITY TO
DETECT THE ENEMY
BORN 1941 – DIED 1953

NIEDERER

Memorial to a beloved ferret.

Courtesy, Abbey Glen Pet Memorial Park.

death. However, using our instinctual common sense, we can find some guidelines from within. We have animal intuition, too, just as our beloved pets do. Wouldn't it be a great sign of respect to try to copy their way of healing? We should not deny the chance to call upon the pet's continuing presence to improve our lives. We are still obliged this much, at least, in living memorial. Our lives must go on, but in a unique way. They are now enriched by the wonderful experience of having shared so much with our beloved companion animals.

CREATING A HEALTHY RELATIONSHIP

Some relationships with pets can become pathological when the owner assumes a distorted sense of responsibility vastly disproportionate to the animals' needs. We have seen many cases where pets are dressed up in different costumes. That can be pure shared fun. But in more extreme examples, they are given dolls or baby toys, and they are even pushed about in small carriages. This behavior gets a bit bizarre and denies their true nature. A strong argument can be made that the pet is being abused by not being permitted to live as an animal. In such instances, we must be concerned with an owner who may be losing a grip on reality, or is expressing unresolved maternal needs and fantasies. This can get serious and may need professional attention.

Single senior citizens who own pets tend to be extremely affectionate. A pet is there to share the older person's loneliness, as well as the changes in the owner's ability to do things. Although the senior's health and mobility may have deteriorated, the pet's love is steadfast. Sometimes very intelligent companion animals realize the changes and make accommodations for them. As hearing, sight and general physical condition diminish, the person's motivation to savor life weakens. Visitors, if any, generally become more scarce, and life becomes a more closed-in experience with the pet. Who can really understand the countless days and years older pet owners must have, talking their lonely hearts out to their pets and disclosing precious memories and dreams? The companion animal shares everything and becomes a very dear and necessary part of the senior's life.

Eventually, when the pet itself shows signs of aging or health deterioration, the owner must become even more of a provider and caretaker. These additional responsibilities can become a real problem to someone who is not functioning well himself. There is a good side to this, however. It makes the older person feel even more vital and needed. On the other hand, when outside assistance is needed, it may feel like a great personal tragedy for the elderly person. The wise, old pet owner can irrationally feel he has failed in his final responsibility to his beloved pet when someone relieves him of those duties.

Usually, senior citizens have one advantage with their advanced age. They have the wisdom that comes with life experience over many years. They have seen friends and family die, and they have learned to become more philosophical. Although their mourning is just as intense for beloved pets, it usually does not last as long. Of course, there are exceptions to this.

A heightened sense of responsibility can be a wonderful part of raising a pet. On the other hand, this responsibility can be taken to destructive extremes. Although commitment spans a wide spectrum of duties, its whole purpose should be justified by the joys and pleasures of the pet's company. When we get too involved with the countless details of the job, we then lose the perspective and joy that is so important for the relationship. The love of a pet should be paramount to all of the other petty details in its stewardship. We have that additional responsibility *to ourselves*.

Case History

A married woman in her early fifties adopted an adorable puppy from the local animal shelter. She and her husband were well-off financially, and therefore they didn't have to work. Her husband thought her attention to the pet was cute, but he wondered if she didn't have other more important things to do now that she was free. She explained that she had a very important sense of responsibility for the puppy's well-being.

The woman became very involved with training the little dog and talked to it as if it were a baby. Her need to be a nurturer again was a very powerful influence. She adored the pet, lavishing so much attention on it that it quickly be-came very spoiled. This made her husband even more upset. Her relationship with their grown children had never been strong, and now they rarely came to visit.

The dog developed a practice of chasing the cars that drove on the isolated street in front of their suburban home. After three years, it was run over and severely injured, with the spine and ribs crushed. The veterinarian had to ask the woman's husband to insist that she allow euthanasia immediately. Although the dog was in intense pain, she could not find the strength to do anything but weep in near hysterics. The husband finally gave his own permission, and the pet was euthanized.

Then the woman withdrew into a severe depression, hating her husband for what he and the veterinarian had done. Their children came to visit and help, but they were rejected, in turn. Although it may have been highly irrational, she felt that her responsibility to the pet had been usurped and that everybody was insensitive to her plight or unwilling to understand.

The real problems, however, had little to do with the dog. That incident was only the trigger mechanism that released long repressed and powerful psychological mechanisms that had never been addressed. She had experienced an emotional breakdown of major proportions.

Rather than counseling for problems only with pet bereavement, intense psychotherapy was called for. Not surprisingly, it turned out that she had suffered from deep feelings of inferiority and insecurity since childhood. Her parents had never let her do anything important by herself. She was never allowed the necessary sense of responsibility one must have to feel successful at anything. People always corrected her, and she developed anxieties about sharing anything, including ideas. Her fear of being criticized or judged made her so vulnerable that she chose to take the offensive in all social situations. Actually, she was afraid of anything she was not able to control.

It took over a year of intense analysis and therapy for her to be able to develop an awareness of her patterns of behavior. It turned out that she had wanted to successfully raise the puppy to make up for her dismal failure in rearing her own children. She really loved them, but she had been in constant dread of failure and criticism. Being an only child herself, with completely insensitive and unresponsive parents, she had nobody to confide in and grew up alone, feeling inferior about everything. When she got married, it was to a man who dominated her, and she even allowed her young children to take on this role with her. Until her breakdown, she had no way to gain perspective on her self-destructive sense of inferiority and aggressive tendencies.

After over a year of intensive psychotherapy, she was able to tentatively establish new relationships with her husband and children. She also realized that her part of her responsibility to her dog should have included its enjoyment and pleasure, rather than worry and fear of criticism in the way she reared it. Of course, that applied to her children, as well. Her condition is very much improved, and she plans to get a new puppy soon.

CHAPTER 3

The

Grieving

Process

Your joy is your sorrow unmasked.

—*Kahlil Gibran*

"How long must I suffer like this?" is one of the first questions asked of bereavement counselors. This is a unique experience that calls for as much help as possible. Generally, deep bereavement may last from a few days to several weeks, depending of course on the person and the circumstances. There is no criterion for how long "normal" grieving takes for anyone. This is something that can never be predicted. But it has been demonstrated in years of study that people mourn much more intensely for someone on whom they were emotionally dependent. Of course, this includes pets.

Some pet owners still fear that it is not socially acceptable to mourn for a pet as they would for a human. This causes enormous internal conflict and disturbing feelings for them because they seem to need approval and support in order to properly grieve for an animal. As a result, these individuals suffer much more than they normally would. Additionally, they run the risk of suppressing these feelings to the point where it could impair the healing process.

A Prayer for Animals

Hear our humble Prayer, O God,
For our friends the animals,
especially for animals who are suffering;
for any that are hunted or lost or deserted or
frightened or hungry,
for all that must be put to death.
We entreat for them all Thy mercy and pity,
and for those who deal with them we ask
a heart of compassion
and gentle hands and kindly words.
Make us, ourselves, to be true friends to animals,
and so to share the blessings of the merciful.

-Albert Schweitzer

A tribute to one who will live on in memory.   *Courtesy, Hartsdale Canine Cemetery, Inc.*

In memory of a cherished bunny.   *Courtesy, Abbey Glen Pet Memorial Park*

In a very real sense, the onset of this bereavement may be regarded as a type of separation anxiety. The well-established patterns of our lives are abruptly terminated by the death of a beloved pet. Suddenly, we are left alone and in a state of shock. The problems that arise can seem overwhelming.

UNDERSTANDING GRIEF AND MOURNING

Understanding the psychological responses and phases of grief and mourning that other people have gone through can help us when we go through this process. This special knowledge can be used to help the grief-stricken mourner get through the worst of it and better understand what is happening.

Many people have a culturally induced fear of grieving and are frightened by being so controlled by death. Because of this they harm themselves emotionally when refusing to allow their real feelings to emerge. But these responses, however suppressed, are real and need to be released in order to heal and come to closure.

Often, a second experience with death is surprisingly more painful than expected. That is because it can stir up repressed and deeprooted psychological problems that were never resolved. Also, the staggering blow of a pet's death can easily trigger other issues that had been long dormant, just beneath the surface of consciousness. This is a matter to be considered by many. The well-trained bereavement counselor should be able to point this out and help arrange other psychological counseling that is specifically directed to this kind of problem.

Grievous mourning is always distinguished by specific psychological reactions. It has been observed that human behavior during this time expresses itself in related phases or stages. This psychological reaction is an evolving process that requires time to complete the healing. However, there are things that the mourner can do to help this process along.

Talking about one's loss and feelings begins the recovery. Pouring out important thoughts and emotions and sharing them with compassionate people is a necessary step in the passage through bereavement. It is important to vent these emotions. It is okay to cry! In fact, it is necessary. Unfortunately, we often see extremes of these responses. On the other hand, many people who are in bereavement for a pet suppress this normal human way of expressing their heartbreak. Repression will almost assuredly create new problems, in addition to the loss already experienced. There are certain basic human emotions that must be released so we can grow past them. Some people need guidance learning this. However, there are those mourners who cannot or will not control their crying, and they unintentionally end up embarrassing or even imposing on anyone near them. Despite overriding grief, we still have social obligations when in the company of others. There are many who feel threatened or even abused by this treatment. Fortunately, we usually have the ability to control these emotions when we are not alone.

The grief and confusion that follow the death of a cherished companion animal need to be better comprehended. When our beloved pets die, we can feel completely out of control, overwhelmed by jumbled feelings of loss and failure—often accompanied by a sense of deep personal guilt, confusion and personal vulnerability. But these are also symptoms of some of the phases of grief that one normally goes through in the process of bereavement.

Personal bereavement for a beloved pet very often is far more intense than is perceived by others. Of course, the degree of mourning and distress is determined by many individual factors, which may be impossible for them to understand. But the pain is so real that it must not be belittled or discounted by anyone, including the self-conscious mourner.

When we live with a dear person or pet for any extended part of our lives, we establish new patterns in our lives and behavior. These become fixed routines and a living part of us and our sense of security. When that person or pet dies, we are suddenly left with an enormous emptiness. Something basic is ripped out of our lives and we are never quite prepared for it. It is a healthy and normal response to experience such intense personal grief at this time.

DIFFERENT REACTIONS TO GRIEF

Men have always had a harder time with strong emotions. This certainly applies to their intensity of feelings during bereavement. They have been conditioned to put on a strong appearance and to give the impression that they are not as emotional as women. But that does not address the reality of how they truly feel. Too often the "macho" image has to be presented, while their hearts are secretly breaking. In Western cultures, even men who have gone through training in "consciousness raising" tend to revert to their instinctive tendencies to maintain their traditional masculine image. It can be a very tough fight within one's self. Men are not supposed to cry or get too emotionally upset. It just doesn't fit the accepted image. Of course, that is nonsense and very self-defeating. Also, the consequences of suppressing these intense feelings can surface later, in many personally damaging ways.

It is interesting to note that although the population of male and female pet owners is about equal, far more women acknowledge their emotional need for support or even counseling. Men will keep their passionate feelings hidden as much as possible. With little means of venting their grief, they tend to find some solace by reading about the subject or observing and identifying with others who are grieving. That activity is safe and secret and does not reveal their perceived emotional "weakness" to anyone. Fortunately, the rapidly increasing public awareness of pet bereavement is making the male's expression of emotional distress a bit easier. But it still takes a lot more soul-searching for men in our culture to grieve as much as they often truly need to.

Depression is a normal human response that can be produced by particularly stressful circumstances. Intense bereavement will produce a whole spectrum of powerful emotions and psychological responses. It is a natural reaction to feel overwhelmed and depressed at this time. Indeed, there would be something very wrong if we did not react this way. We are normally depressed at the loss of anything we hold dear. This includes our habits, patterns of behavior and even our possessions. If a torn jacket, an unfavorable report, a smashed-up bike or a dented car can depress us, certainly the loss of a beloved pet should do at least the same.

THE PHASES OF GRIEF

Since the late 1960s, starting with Elizabeth Kubler-Ross, a few pioneering Western psychologists and sociologists began to make a science of studying the psychology of humans during bereavement. These professionals discovered that there are regular, predictable phases that all normal people must pass through during intense mourning to get over their grief. This is nature's way of helping us to heal psychologically from such an emotional blow, and the process must run its course to be effective.

These phases or stages were identified, listed and studied intensively. It was quickly realized that they are universal to all humans raised in Western culture. After suffering the death of a beloved one, this process is a normal and predictable healing reaction of the mind and should not be interfered with. Mourners are counseled to face their grief, however intense or debilitating it may be. One has to *live through* the pain to get past it. Because it is a normal response to avoid grief and suffering, this kind of psychological healing is especially difficult and requires time. Making a recovery that results in emotional stability is a gradual process and needs a great deal of patience, as well.

People who resist or even suppress their transition through these stages always create more complex problems that will continue to distress them. It was learned that the only way to remedy the situation is to address the unresolved problems. This can be accomplished even after many years of suffering, which could have been prevented.

These stages are different and transitional, and they may appear simultaneously or in a different sequence than listed here. Although they usually *do* unfold in the order given, each will appear in due course and then fade away, if resolved. There is nothing to worry about if you perceive a shifting in the sequence. Nature has provided us with a natural beginning, middle and end to all of this. Going with the flow will heal you.

Slightly differing names and sequences for these stages or phases have been suggested by some writers. For our purposes here, we have found it most effective to work with these, which are examined in the next six chapters:

Shock and Disbelief	Chapter 4
Anger, Alienation and Distancing	Chapter 5
Denial	Chapter 6
Guilt	Chapter 7
Depression	Chapter 8
Resolution (Closure)	Chapter 9

Some counselors prefer naming *grief* as an additional stage. This is not used here because it is believed that the term is too general. Grieving is so personal that it cannot be clearly defined without becoming vague or generalized. It can be seen as our natural, overall emotional response while progressing through all phases of bereavement. Since each of us has such unique reactions and responses to death, it is necessary to examine each of these stages in some detail. The following chapters will guide you in this.

GRIEF IS A NATURAL RESPONSE

Intense grief is not an expression of extreme or abnormal behavior. Nor is it an indication of a neurosis or disorder. It is a natural response to sudden, overwhelming loss, and it runs a normal course within wide margins. It is considered normal as long as the grieving person is not in any danger of harming him- or herself or anyone else, and if it does not persist for an unnaturally long time. Support and tender loving care are what mourners need most while working their way through this heartache.

People have so many differences in personality and the way that they are affected that it is not possible to predict how everyone will react through these stages. Thus, we have to deal with each as it arises. There are many factors that can affect us when dealing with our bereavement. These variables include: past experience with grief and/or death; individual personality differences and histories; degree and quality of social support; spiritual, religious and ethnic background; cultural influences; age and gender; and the special nature of the lost relationship. It is of great help to gain insights into these variables. The best ways to achieve greater insight are through counseling, self-analysis, reading and networking with others who have suffered this type of loss.

A beloved pet becomes part of the human companion. When the pet dies, it becomes the end of an era in that person's life. This death shockingly marks the forced close of one stage and the beginning of the next. But each next stage is based on the strengths and weaknesses of the last. Certainly the loving memory of the pet remains with us as we live and grow on. Each time a beloved pet dies it is like a painful metamorphosis in the life of the owner. Each successive stage allows the mourner to become wiser with age, better and more seasoned with treasured memories and experiences. Pain and experience are fundamental to personal growth and wisdom.

It must be mentioned here that there will always be some future emotional aftershocks, long past the period of bereavement. However well adjusted and healed we may be, our loving memories are still there within us. They are just not as obvious as before. It is a normal psychological response to occasionally re-experience some of the tears and heartache we lived through earlier. Such love is never forgotten or lost. Fortunately, it is not as debilitating as before. Going through the transitional phases of bereavement makes this possible.

Some survivors of great personal tragedy tend to be stoic in their behavior, especially when it comes to death. As mentioned, these people also may be inclined to suppress rather than accept their feelings and will not willingly resolve their grief through mourning. And there are others who feel a need to experience their sense of guilt as self-punishment. Their real problems are not perceived by others, and they are in great need of professional psychological counseling.

Too many well-intentioned people enjoy playing the psychologist. They can cause unintentional harm, making the person who is grieving feel apologetic, defensive or even defective. With inappropriate intervention, well-intentioned people often try to create the false impression that everything is fine and that time is the only thing necessary for healing. Any misguided advice can cause the suppression of normal grief responses. That will harm the process that must be painfully worked through before resolution can be achieved. Despite their good hearts, they are untrained and unaware of potential problems that could be damaging.

Generally, it is unwise to intervene in anyone's mourning process. Offering impressive psychological terminology and explanations may tend to scare the already upset mourner, when he or she is not in a position to see things as they really are. They may be pressed into feeling that they are "losing it," although this intense behavior may be a normal expression for some individuals at the time.

Case History

One of my patients was a widow whose dog died four years before she came to me. When the woman's husband died a few years before the dog, she was shaken, but seemed to stand up well to the shock. She described the mourning period as brief and well-handled. To her it was very important to keep up appearances for the neighbors.

She tried very hard to put on a brave face. All her attention and love focused on her dog, who reveled in this. As the years went on, the woman grew increasingly dependent on what the dog represented to her. It was made into a combination of surrogate roles, from child to best friend to husband.

When the dog died a few years later, she was overwhelmed by inconsolable grief and even had to be hospitalized for a few days. After an intense period of mourning, which was never resolved, she tried to go about a normal way of life, but she couldn't without the dog. She would not get another pet, and as a result, her life became entirely devoted to the remembrance of her deceased dog. Her apartment was turned into a near shrine, with pictures draped in black and the dog's toys and other memorabilia on prominent display. The pet's ashes and urn occupied the central focus of the living room.

The woman continued this way for a few more years in perpetual unresolved mourning and grief. She was finally referred to me. After analysis, it turned out that much of this abnormal behavior had been in response to other deep-rooted problems she had never faced or resolved. She suffered a deep sense of guilt for not having grieved for her husband as much as she felt she was supposed to and was afraid of letting any feelings get out of hand, so she suppressed them. Thus, she could never complete the mourning process for her husband or for the dog.

Later, she admitted to another major complication. It turned out that early in her marriage she had a baby who died in an auto accident, when he was only a year old. She had never forgiven herself or her husband for that, and it was a psychological time bomb just waiting to explode. She had been through two deaths that had affected her greatly, but only after the loss of her beloved dog did she react emotionally. That was the trigger mechanism that set everything off at once.

Her healing depended on dragging out old and very painful memories and working on each of them. It was critical that she identify and resolve her suppressed feelings of worthlessness and guilt, which she had never been able to admit to herself. Her therapy was long and difficult, taking a few years, but there is a happy ending to the story. She now is living a normal life after having wasted so many precious years. And she is beginning to socialize again, although shy about meeting men. Two cats live with her as her loving companions and constant support.

Case History

A young man in his mid-twenties called me, explaining on the telephone that his dog had died about a week before and he was much more upset than he should be. He tried to appear in control, but it was clear that he was very upset. Not surprisingly, he readily accepted the suggestion to come in for a private session.

He was a rookie cop in the New York City Police Department, married for about three years. His father had also been a cop and was a hard, insensitive man who never allowed him or his brothers to cry. That was only for girls, they were told. His dog, a fourteen-year-old Golden Retriev-er, had been with him since his teens and was almost like a sibling to him. It was old, weak and half-blind, and it had fallen down a flight of stairs, severely injuring itself. He had to have the beloved pet immediately euthanized. "I thought I was losing it," he told me, describing his heartache.

His young wife was sympathetic, but she could not share his profound bereavement. She was in the last month of her first pregnancy and had other things that concerned her more. He had nobody close who could really understand and had no way to identify and express his anguish. At work he was "one of the boys," trying to make and live up to a reputation of being a tough cop—a "real male." His friends at the precinct were all very "macho," and he was always trying to gain the approval of his veteran partner, an older man who hated weakness of any kind.

He didn't dare expose his feelings of grief and mourning for the dog, feeling certain they would either poke fun at him or think him a wimp, undeserving of their camaraderie or respect. But he realized that something terrible was going on, deep in his head and heart. Even during work he was in a state of emotional distress and tension. He thought about going to a departmental psychologist, but feared the embarrassment he thought that could instigate. He knew that he needed some sort of help, and he had no close friends who could share and commiserate with him in his mourning. In addition, his pastor had discounted his bereavement for a dog, saying that the grief would go away by itself soon.

In two sessions he was able to have a good overview of what the bereavement process was like, especially for him. We also discussed his need to hide his feelings, especially when his manhood felt threatened by their exposure. Al-though these few consultations were not enough to cure all his problems, they established a better sense of understanding and self-assurance. We explored ways he could share his feelings with others who had already experienced the same grief. We also discussed the effect that "macho" attitude had on him and how he could learn to address that in the future. He was able to face his grief and pass through the period of mourning with less emotional chaos. "This was the foothold I needed," he said and decided to start private psychotherapy to help work on other personal problems, as well. "Everything is connect-ed," he said.

CHAPTER 4

Shock
and
Disbelief

O, aching time! O, moments big as years!

—John Keats

S hock and disbelief are the first likely responses to the death of a
beloved pet. This early stage may last from a few hours to even
a few days. During this time we suffer from a loss of a sense of
awareness and proportion in dealing with things. It is especially difficult when we first experience this emotional overload— and usually
cannot even begin to grip the reality of the situation. The mind is
stunned by powerful psychological reactions that can completely
overwhelm what feeble emotional strengths we may have at the time.
We respond at this stage with a physical or mental numbness that
may feel overwhelming. Basic experiences and information related to
the death can be "blocked out" and not remembered, just as if they
never happened.

Counselors trained in human bereavement are familiar with situations in which the question, "Is he or she really dead?" is repeated
over and over, despite very specific information or proof. Disbelief is

An epitaph for a beautiful young lion.   *Courtesy, Hartsdale Canine Cemetery, Inc.*

a powerful temporary defense. There is a more familiar situation demonstrating disbelief, though. We are all familiar with the common expression beginning with "I can't believe...." At least in this application the speaker is able to accept the reality, even though it seems terrible or even fantastic.

RESPONDING TO A SHOCK

In extreme instances, the mind may respond to a shock by becoming completely oblivious to the situation. It may refuse to accept any input that supports the traumatic news. It is as if a person were hypnotized and instructed to totally ignore certain stimuli.

This response of numbness is the mind's way of protecting itself from having to handle too much too soon after the initial shock and impact of the death. It is nature's last defense that shields us from the violence to the mind that can be caused by unbearable stimuli.

There is a similarity between extreme examples of shock and disbelief and some forms of amnesia. The mind has fantastic defenses. In some cases of child abuse, for example, the child's memories of the offense are completely blocked out. Only rarely does the person recall the offense, and that is only after many years have gone by. The child could be middle-aged or older before even beginning to have any recollection of what really happened.

The mind also plays similar tricks on people suffering from multiple personalities. Because they cannot handle stress, nearly any sudden shock or strain will shift them into an invented personality that can deal with such a situation. In staggering under the initial shock, the mind is buying time to be able to live with a situation that is otherwise unbearable.

Shock is sometimes the first sign of a post-traumatic stress syndrome, such as strong bereavement. When the initial reactions of shock and disbelief wear off, an overwhelming torrent of other strong emotional responses will follow. This flood of emotion is full of distortions and misperceptions at first. Time will help with the healing, and we must be patient with ourselves, despite how difficult that may seem to be at the moment. Normally, these strange and unpleasant reactions will run their course and fade, as part of the mourning process.

We need to keep in mind that we are dealing with the sudden onset of human tragedy. There is really no way to prepare defenses against shock and disbelief. Powerful emotions, intense reactions and feelings, a sense of violation and utter helplessness and distress can prevail for a while.

We tend not to heal from bereavement as quickly as we would from other adversities because we may be going through separation anxiety that has come about abruptly. In this particular situation, normal patterns of daily living are broken, and we have no other routines that can carry us through. Sometimes the structure of going to work or being seriously involved in some activity will provide the necessary means to keep us going while our inner resources have a chance to rebuild themselves.

There will be times, in the depths of our misery during bereavement, when we will suffer intensely, indeed. Because of this extreme response it is not uncommon for people in bereavement to wonder about their sanity. Yet we must realize that there is a difference between this normal, temporary agony and one that may not ease within a reasonable period of time.

Acute grief, also referred to as exaggerated grief, is not an expression of any normal mourning process. This kind of overreaction is somewhat easy to identify. Some of its many possible symptoms are intensified irritability and sleeplessness, or even their opposites— extreme withdrawal and fatigue. Other indications may be excessive anger, antisocial behavior or persistent nightmares. Sometimes one will experience near-hallucinations, such as hearing or seeing glimpses of the deceased pet.

Too often an abnormal response to this post-traumatic stress syndrome is overlooked as something that will eventually go away. Unfortunately, it does seem to disappear, but it does not really go away. It becomes repressed and will possibly fester for the rest of this person's life. There must be a release. Professional help is definitely needed in this case.

The best generalization that can be made about acute or exaggerated grief is that it is suffered by people who are least able to cope with it and probably already emotionally injured and suffering from other major stresses in their lives. The weight of bereavement can become the proverbial straw that breaks the camel's back.

In bereavement, a normal amount of shock and disbelief are reasonable responses and should not prove too distressing in their own right. These responses fade and pass fairly quickly. We all experience this to some degree. Usually this response is an accurate measure of the emotional intensity that will be expressed in the bereavement stages that are yet to follow.

Case History

A single woman in her early thirties went on a month-long vacation to Europe. She left her dog with a reputable and expensive boarding kennel. When she returned, she was informed that her dog died of sudden heart failure about a week after her departure. Since there had been no way of contacting her, the body was cremated and the ashes kept for her return.

She grew furious at the news and refused to accept it as the truth. She was certain that there must be a conspiracy and felt that her dog must be alive somewhere. Talks with the veterinarians who tried to save the dog and the managers of the kennel and crematorium only intensified her anger and disbelief. She tried, in vain, to call in the police. Then she tried to retain a lawyer, who attempted to advise her about her denial of what had to be reality. This only served to further distress her to the point where she could not even go back to work until she received what she deemed to be satisfaction.

A close friend persuaded her to come into therapy for just an initial meeting. Fortunately, we were able to strike a rapport with each other. Follow-up sessions established that she felt totally responsible and guilty for having set up the selfish conditions of her absence during this critical time.

We discussed shock and denial, and the truth began to seep in. She quickly lapsed into a deep depression, during which it became necessary for a psycho-pharmacologist to prescribe specific drug therapy to be used in conjunction with her psychotherapy sessions.

Fortunately, she was able to return to work in about two weeks, and she slowly recovered afterward. Prior to that well-needed vacation, other stresses in her life had been tearing her apart emotionally. The death of her beloved dog was the trigger mechanism that set her off into shock and denial. She now sees this and is working at self-improvement in normal psychotherapy sessions. The prognosis is good.

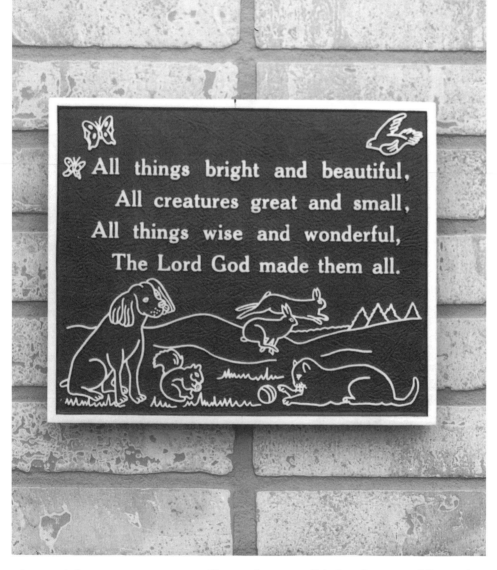

All things bright and beautiful,
All creatures great and small,
All things wise and wonderful,
The Lord God made them all.

A prayer in bronze.

Photograph courtesy of Matthews International Corporation

CHAPTER 5

Anger, Alienation and Distancing

Freeze, freeze, thou bitter sky,
thou dost not bite as nigh
as benefits forgot.
Though thou the waters warp
thy sting is not as sharp
as friends remembered not.

—William Shakespeare

*T*he anger stage is a distraught temporary response to an overwhelming sense of frustration and outrage. It can take many forms, but it is always easily recognizable. Sometimes our suffering makes us feel as though we have to lash out at someone else, anyone. We are ingenious at creating impassioned justifications for re-directing the rage within us. In this stage, it is very difficult to cope rationally with disappointing people and situations. We can spread this anger in all directions, almost at random.

ACTING OUT ANGER

From a state of total responsibility and control of the pet's life we are suddenly plunged into a condition of absolute helplessness and despair. We sense that, somehow, this death should not have happened, and God, fate or something we personally depended on has betrayed us. The absolute nature of death leaves us no bargaining chips. We are totally helpless. This is in stark contrast to the freedom we had in making all decisions before the pet's life was snatched away from us. Suddenly, we have been made helpless and useless, and this is unbearably frustrating. It is a normal, temporary response to react with passion at being suddenly checkmated by death. However, most of us have trouble expressing anger at others because we are not effective in using it. When we are suddenly immersed in the passions of bereavement, this difficulty becomes much more complicated and upsetting.

Any remotely involved person or authority can be transformed into a scapegoat by someone needing to do this. Because of the veterinarian's dominant role in the pet's life and death, the hospital and medical staff are usually the most assailable and the first to be blamed. They may be completely without guilt, but at this time we are in a blind passion to dump our anger on someone or something, anything!

When the life of a beloved pet is suddenly ended, we can momentarily lose our perspective of right and wrong. People or situations that could be considered even remotely blamable will be condemned, however irrational this may seem at another time. Frustration and rage, aggravated by a violent sense of loss, can distort our perspective and sense of right and wrong. In our passionate need to assign blame at this stage of the mourning process, tiny incidents that would normally have been overlooked can be blown up into exaggeration and misconstruction.

Anger can express itself in amazing forms. It may be turned outward, just as easily as inward. It is a normal human response to blame ourselves for all kinds of imagined weaknesses and faults in frustration at not being able to prevent this death. Being forewarned, though, can sometimes take the keen edge off this response. It is a loss of control that we had taken entirely for granted. We even might feel anger at our own survival after the pet's death. This frequently leads to depression, and we need tender loving care, rather than rebuttal. An angry attack is not likely to produce a sympathetic response in anyone. It becomes an irrational exercise in frustration and personal rage, while trying to cope with the fury at being made so helpless and cheated by death.

Sometimes we are so angry at ourselves that we create social situations that become intolerable to others. Overreactions and inappropriate anger can be inducements to being punished, which may be just what some bereavers are unconsciously asking for to satisfy feelings of unresolved guilt. This type of neurotic response is not uncommon, but it is almost always self-destructive to some degree. We cruelly punish ourselves by unnecessarily burning bridges behind us. This irrational action is related to temper tantrums in children.

For your own sake, you must eventually get control of this erratic expression of your passion. How long can you sustain and justify such an emotional drain on yourself, when it is not really clear what or who is at fault? And behavior, there is always present a strong sense of self-blame and betrayal is always present, which confuses the bereaver even more.

Completely suppressed anger can become a self-destructive force. It needs to be identified and vented to enable you to let it go. This is an intensely personal, subjective response. Confronting anger is very difficult, and it requires you to be absolutely candid with yourself. You and your pain deserve better treatment than keeping anger submerged and unresolved. But first, we must try to make it more objective and honest.

The following offers a very effective method to help yourself. It should take at least a few sittings for you to finish this exercise and find it useful. Do not try to do it all at one sitting. You need time to think it over and gradually complete it.

Make a list headed "Anger." Number each response individually. Skip a line between each response.

1. Write the names of people you are very angry with. Do not include yourself here.

2. Make a list of the names of others you feel have upset you, in lesser ways, in your bereavement. They may be the next victims of your anger.

39

3. After you have finished the list, go back and fill in the reasons for each person's "guilt."

4. Make another list of the names of institutions, situations or anything else you feel is responsible for causing you unnecessary pain in your bereavement.

5. Make a final list. Head it "Me." Enumerate any reasons for feeling anger at yourself.

Then put these lists away for at least a few hours before adding to them or reading them again. That short span of time can give you greater objectivity. In a few days, rewrite all the lists, neatly organizing any added comments. This will help you a great deal.

A CLEAR PERSPECTIVE

There is no question that you hurt and that your terrible loss might have been more clearly understood by people who should know better. Yes, there are always some insensitive ones who upset you with their callousness or stupid comments about your bereavement. Yet, was there something valid in their lives that prevented them from understanding the death you now face? Are they unable to cope with your problems, or are they acting out their own? And are you now, by getting so involved and angry, attempting to make their inadequacies your new problems, as well? Get your perspectives straight.

Are you really looking for any "peg" just to hang your anger on? When will you be willing (or ready) to try to forgive? Was the veterinarian *really* at fault, or is that part of your emotional need to blame someone or something? Sometimes, when we hurt most, we want to strike out at family and others who are closest, if they failed to help us when we needed them most. A secret cry for love and understanding can turn into a confused sense of "justifiable rage" and "righteous indignation."

Role-practice your anger, acting it out with your analyst (if you have one) or a close friend. If you are fortunate enough to have some kind of support group, try this with them: Ask someone else to take your part, understanding how much and why you are hurt by each of the people represented on the list you just made. One at a time, act out the reasoning of each person on your list, and discuss this with the others present, until you feel complete satisfaction. Consider any possible excuses the people on the list might have to offer, even if you think they are really at fault. Listen to what the others may be saying. Be fair. There is a lot to be learned about yourself and your needs from this kind of objectivity. It will help you ease your pain.

Might there be legitimate reasons you didn't see, for the people that you listed as being unable to meet your needs at this time? Could it be that death secretly scares them, and they cannot handle your situation? Maybe there is something else just as terrible in their lives that you are not aware of. Is it possible that your frustration, pain and disappointment are not letting you accept *their* problems and human frailty? Perhaps your grief and shock are making you lose perspective of things for the time being. We can become very narrow-minded and selfish during bereavement. It is too easy to become judgmental of others and act out inappropriately at this time.

Is it possible that your anger is disproportionate and twisting things a bit? What is it really about? Could it possibly be directed at yourself? Maybe it is your own rotten luck or just hard times. Maybe you blame the establishment, your parents or your spouse. There are so many people and situations that can affect and upset our lives. Respond candidly and as frankly as you can to this self-examination. Are you overreacting? That is a probable sign that something else is unconsciously troubling you. When this happens, it is easy to mistakenly identify problems or responses. It is nearly impossible to think clearly and without distortion when anger is present.

RESPONSES FROM OTHERS

Friends, family, colleagues, religion. Where do they come in? Were there any true attempts by them to help you? Were your expectations of them realistic, knowing their real capacity as you do? Or were you really hoping more than expecting? Were they able to share your privacy? Or perhaps you felt they invaded it? Maybe you didn't want to let them touch your secret vulnerability and grief. Did you seem demanding or imposing to them? Are you really able to explain and share your pain? If not, how could you blame others for not crossing the impossible barrier you set up?

Rash actions are easily justified at the moment, but they are almost always regretted. Too often, they cannot be erased later, to our enormous sorrow. In our passion we can all too easily lose perspective of what is good or bad for ourselves. What is the point in being self-destructive when we are really trying so desperately to help ourselves? A moment's outburst, however good it feels at that instant, is not worth it.

It is easy to be caught off-balance by those who seem rash and judgmental about our grief. Who among us has not heard the comment that one shouldn't be so upset because, "It was only a cat (or dog)?" Or perhaps you've been told that your problem would be over if you just got another one right away. What do they really know about you and your dear pet's death? How dare they be so insensitive?

But these people are trying to make what they think is a legitimate point from their limited perspectives. We can call them stupid, but does that make them bad? They just cannot seem to accept bereavement for a pet, and thus come up very short of our needs and expectations at this terrible time. It hurts even more during this grief, when our emotional reserve of strength is especially low.

But we also may have met up with some truly insensitive, nasty or even cruel people who find pleasure in inflicting pain on others. They prey on the most vulnerable victims they can find, and anyone bereaving for a pet is just right for them. An angry response to this sort of social misfit is well-deserved. But spending too much time on this behavior is really a waste of your vital energy. Your reaction really won't affect them at all. And you have more important things that require your emotions and feelings. Scorn these people, if you will, but walk away from them.

Our Responses to Others

At this time, our normal response to such frustration is to become angry, perhaps even enough to justify alienation, feeling as though we never want to see or have anything to do with that person again. When we are irrational or petulant, we tend to take dramatic steps that are most often regretted later. But then that may be too late. Being too quick on the draw is usually dangerous and final.

We are off-balance at a vulnerable time like this, and we tend to seek any outlet for all our powerful emotions. It becomes easy to justify vilifying someone who hurts us now. But we must not go on burning our bridges behind us. Some of the personal relationships that seem strained at this upsetting time have real value and positive significance in our lives. It can be very self-defeating to feel insulted by these people. We want to show our anger by punishing them.

Distancing or permanently alienating ourselves from them, however, may not serve our real purposes. Also, in turn, they may not forgive us. This would be a foolish, preventable loss.

These people may see pets as possessions, childish playthings and nearly frivolous wastes of time and expense. Or they could be very upset and threatened by the hidden meanings of death, which they refuse to confront with you. They may become agitated and short with you for lavishing all of your sensitivity on a pet's death, when it is too frightening for them to contemplate the thought of death at all. This probably is somewhat intimidating to them and their inadequate grasp of the subject. Their defensive behavior may seem rude, belittling or even hostile. But maybe they felt you were the pushy one. In responding to this kind of disappointment, it is too easy to be impatient and overreact with hasty, disturbed and powerful emotions.

Some people who are close to us may not offer any response at all to our bereavement. The resulting silence or absence of a meaningful statement can be too easily mistaken as a critical comment. Very often, persons make this kind of non-response because they just do not know how to reply. Death is a frightening thing. They may well be unable to discuss the subject without feeling greatly threatened. If you love or respect them, despite your own breaking heart and need for support, don't push. They are human, too.

TYPES OF RESPONSES

You can make three basic types of responses to a perceived assault on your grief: The first is to strike back quickly, with bitterness and immediate anger. As mentioned earlier, in some rare cases this may be very well-deserved. The second is to be caught so far off-guard that you don't know what to say. Your confused or embarrassed response can probably give the impression that you are not really contradicting or disagreeing. Sometimes a person in authority, such as a boss or supervisor, may have you at this disadvantage if you are not ready to handle it. The third and most effective response is to be prepared. You can look a reasonable but insensitive person right in the eye and say something like, "You don't have a pet and can't possibly understand what kind of love and understanding there was for me. How can you judge my grief? That hurts and offends me. If you have any respect for me, please be more tolerant when such deep, personal feelings are involved!"

These are only some examples of non-threatening responses to the challenge of the situation. It is very important not to force anyone into a corner. This approach can maintain the respect you might otherwise lose. And it may keep you in control of the situation. Also, this kind of unexpected logic might quite possibly elicit an insight that the person could not have reached otherwise. It probably will help to save a valuable relationship. And lastly, it also may prevent additional unnecessary suffering for yourself.

It can be difficult to remain cool and not react to the perceived hurt and insensitivity all around us at this vulnerable time. But it is encouraging to realize that this emotional turmoil is a stage, and will pass more easily if we express our feelings to caring and sympathetic listeners. Friends and pet support groups are the best medicine at this time.

Anger is a highly personalized, emotional response to a perceived offense or violation. It has many legitimate uses as well as abuses. But what valid purpose can it serve in memorializing a beloved life that has been snatched away? Can we be angry at death or the reality of things? Can we be angry at ourselves for not being able to defeat death? Fortunately, this response is only temporary, and it will pass.

Eventually, we must accept the new reality without the beloved pet. We have reached the bottom line. Since death knows no bargaining, we must come to terms with ourselves and our loss. There is no other way.

Case History

A seventeen-year-old boy was referred to me when he started experiencing strong anger and feelings of alienation with many people close to him after the death of his beloved dog. She was fourteen, and the two grew up together as extremely close pals—almost siblings. She needed to have a tumor removed and though the vet had explained the potential dangers of general anesthesia for older dogs, the boy felt it was necessary. He also opted to have her teeth cleaned while she was under. Unfortunately, the dog died on the table.

The boy was devastated and went through shock, disbelief and fury at the veterinarian and her technicians, trying unsuccessfully to pick fault with anything they might have done wrong. In need of compassion, he turned to the people closest to him, but his adored married sister made no extra efforts to console him. In his grief, he swore he would never speak with her again. He was co-captain of his high school track team, and the coach he had worshipped belittled his grief and told him that he was "acting like a baby" and that "It's time to become a man." In addition to these disappointments, his girlfriend suggested that he just get another dog. The boy was in an intense emotional crisis and was angry and hurt. He felt let down by these close people he had relied most on. He was referred to me by his concerned parents, who could not reason with him.

Fortunately, this young man was bright and open to new ideas. He had not believed his dog would die and was totally unwilling to accept feelings of his own guilt. In therapy, he tried to consider the people who had so bitterly disappointed him, and he admitted that his sister had experienced troubles with the death of her father-in-law and couldn't even go to the funeral. As much as she loved her brother, she could not handle even the death of his dog, and she avoided discussing it with him.

He had to learn to accept that his coach was not the sensitive man he had idealized, which was hard to do. But he did not act on his immediate impulse to damn this man and quit the team. (The next semester he won a statewide competition, with the guidance of this same coach.) And he had to learn the hard way that his girlfriend was not really his soul mate. They actually had little in common, especially a love of animals. It was ironic, but the insensitive coach was right in insisting the boy had to become a man. Of course, there were other more caring and acceptable ways he should have expressed that.

It was a difficult year for the boy, but in just a few sessions he was able to understand why these people were not able to be there for him during his bereavement. He was forced to do a lot of growing up, unfortunately at the especially terrible time of his pet loss. But after working to understand his feelings of anger and alienation, he was able to get through the period of mourning and social realignment within just a few weeks. Growing up has its painful moments, and his grief and bereavement were aggravated by these other emotional disappointments.

Learning about the different stages of mourning helped him greatly, especially gaining a perspective on his feelings of alienation and distancing. His healing was quite rapid, but of course he was never the same, which he seemed to regret at first. He would have liked another dog, but he was going to an out-of-town college the next year. He wisely decided to get one at another time in the future.

CHAPTER 6

Denial

Parting is all we know of heaven and all we need of hell.

—Emily Dickinson

enial is one of the earliest stages of mourning. It is easily confused with disbelief, which accompanies the shock of first learning about the death (see Chapter 4). Actually, denial is something of a modification of disbelief, and there are some psychologists who tend to lump these two terms together as minor variations of the same response.

But all this fancy hairsplitting and defining is of no value at all to the deeply bereaved individual who is full of pain. For our purposes here, we will consider that in the first stage of shock, we still have not had time to accept the reality. We simply refuse to believe. That is disbelief. Denial, on the other hand, usually develops a little bit later, and in this stage we resentfully acknowledge that the death has taken place. At the same time, however, we look for ways to refute it. Denial is rooted in fantasy and a passionate hope for wish-fulfillment.

FANTASY

When overwhelmed by the terribly upsetting finality of death, we are strongly tempted to deny reality. There is a natural tendency to still crave that somehow it was a bad dream or some kind of terrible hallucination. We very much want to believe that our pet is not really dead. Passionately, we hope it might all be okay again. This sweet

"One Small Furry Friend" bronze plaque. *Photograph courtesy of Matthews International Corporation*

"Come to me."

Courtesy, Abbey Glen Pet Memorial Park

fantasy removes us a little from the pain we are going through. But gradually the grim reality will set back in. The life of the pet is over, gone, ended! The pain is with us now. Denial is usually a brief stage, and fortunately it is over quickly. But when it is acute or prolonged, there is little most people can do to ease it for anyone else. The person in acute denial needs professional help.

We live in what can be termed a euphemistic society. It prefers indirect references to unpleasant words or concepts and tends to avoid certain aspects of reality. It also conditions us to try to redesign reality a bit. In our Western culture, we are nurtured in the belief that "wishing might make it so." The fairy tales and other types of stories we knew as children were filled with plots in which the good were sometimes given a second chance to escape from death or harm. As such, magic and romantic reverie were at the core of our early emotional development. That stays with us all of our lives as a delightful remembrance of childhood experience and innocence. The human brain retains everything it ever experiences, and as a result, during times of intense stress the psyche will call upon its vast data bank for some sort of refuge. That is why denial is termed an escape mechanism. This impulse is so powerful that if there is no such memory or idea, the mind will immediately create one. But the childlike tendency to believe and trust in miracles and fairy tale endings still exists in us. Cartoon characters are never killed or hurt. We have been conditioned to be able to believe that if we all clap our hands at that right moment, Tinkerbell will live again. We may think that if we wish or pray strongly enough, maybe, just maybe, our beloved pets will be okay. But of course, it doesn't work.

This analogy applies to all other aspects of life, as well. As adults we are often confronted with shocking circumstances beyond our control. We have learned many ways to avoid or even accept such situations. But there are times when we can do nothing about them. We can seem like pawns in a chess game. Once death has taken over, it is too late, despite our hope and fantasy and the powerful effects they have on us.

The innocent child within each of us naturally craves a happy ending. Knowledge and learning about death are so carefully avoided that we can never be really prepared. And it does come to all living things, despite our fancies and most fervent prayers. We are never ready for this grim reality.

Sometimes we need to regress to a fantasy and childlike state of make-believe. As in fairy tales, most kinds of magic are supposed to perform wonderful things. Oh, how we want to believe! For example, if we put out the food dish, maybe somehow our pet will come to eat. This is a lovely reverie, but it is not real. We have to let go. The death is over and done with, and we are being carried onward in the stream of life and daily responsibilities. The pet has died, time is passing and we must go on. We have to stop clinging to passionate memories and learn to incorporate them as loving components of our new lives.

DEFENSE MECHANISMS

Psychological defense mechanisms play a very important part in maintaining mental stability. Initial denial has the specific function of immediately delaying the full emotional impact of a reality that is very upsetting. It temporarily limits the damage that trauma can produce. It serves as a protective means to put us in some sort of painless limbo for a while. Normally, denial in bereavement lasts only a short while. Other realities quickly close in, forcing us back to the facts of the death and our private loss. As painful as it is, we are going through the necessary developmental stages of the mourning-healing process. Denial is part of a transitional state in our personal metamorphosis.

In understanding some of the fantastic capabilities of the human mind, it is not really surprising to learn that there is another form of denial we can experience. Delayed denial is more given to contemplation than initial denial. It comes later, usually after the body of the pet has been provided for and all the other immediate responsibilities have been taken care of. It seems to crop up when we are alone, smothered by grief, frustration, rage and a sense of helplessness. The pet's presence is still very strong, and we still unconsciously expect a greeting at the door when we come home. The apartment or house seems too empty. It doesn't seem real. Occasional mild hallucinations are not uncommon. At this stage, we may sometimes think we heard or saw a fleeting glimpse of the pet. This can be upsetting, almost as if reality has gone through some sort of time warp. And, despite our logic, we hope that things might somehow revert to the way they were. Maybe the pet really isn't dead—or doesn't have to stay that way. Maybe if we try to make some bargain with God the pet will come back again. Therefore, in this early stage we create the psychological need and function for what is termed *bargaining*. Sometimes this plays a much more impassioned role even before death actually happens, if it is anticipated. We need to be aware that bargaining doesn't ever work. But now it is after the fact. And a fact it remains. All our tears and wishing cannot wash it out or change it.

Despite that unpleasant and cruel reality, it is a very normal response to grasp at anything that could possibly bring back the beloved pet. During intense grief, logic does not influence all of our thinking and feeling. We would give anything to correct that tragic occurrence. Why not employ intensive prayer and personal renunciation of certain very personal aspects of our lives? Wouldn't God see how earnest and genuine we are and possibly make some sort of exception? We have been raised to believe that miracles have occurred, so why not one now?

Bargaining is often attempted, but it is never successful. Distraught people can be ingenious in their sincerity and variations on this theme. Some mourners who are stuck in their bereavement will set up a whole new lifestyle, one that calls for dramatic change, sacrifice and self-denial. This is presumably for the edification, and appeasement, of God to bring about that beseeched miracle. Unfortunately, such conduct is bad for several reasons: It doesn't work; it reinforces a deep sense of guilt; it ruins one's life; and it passionately avoids truth and reality. Actually, a state of prolonged self-immobilization is caused by other deep, underlying problems that had never been resolved and desperately need to be addressed. The loss of the beloved pet is not the real issue here. This is pathological behavior and it desperately needs professional help.

Most people would love to believe in magic. All our lives we have heard of many forms of this amazing practice. Admittedly, most of it is slight-of-hand entertainment. But there always have been examples we could never explain. Why couldn't there be some kind of magic that could work for us, in this terrible need? The more we become educated about the ways of the world, the more we begin to realize how little we really know or understand. It may be possible that there are wonders awaiting us, if only we knew how to comprehend them. The entire history of civilization is filled with examples of this search. Magic has never been proved, and by the same argument, it has never been disproved. But for now, in our pain and need, all we can do is hope and escape into fantasy. We will resort to almost anything at this time. The potential reward is worth it.

People who did not personally witness the death more commonly fantasize about it still being alive somehow. Pet owners who have to be told about their demise while they had been away frequently have a more difficult time accepting the immediate reality. The shock of having to be informed about something so intensely personal can ag-gravate the problem. This appalling end to such a very close relationship is announced by a stranger, who is an unwelcome third party to this very personal relationship. That feels wrong, somehow. It is almost like some kind of defilement of a secret and intimate covenant. Here, the message is often rejected, along with the messenger.

Most veterinarians have developed an awareness of this situation through experience and common sense. Today, all veterinary colleges and teaching hospitals are finally offering sensitivity training to their personnel. They have found that it is important to have pet owners actually see the body, if they can. This visual impact and confirmation helps acceptance of what had been just words and abstractions during intense emotion. The newly bereaved pet owner is then best served by having some private time, alone, with the body. The first grief should be private and together, if possible.

Seeing the pet's body can be overwhelming for some people, and they need to maintain some slight distance emotionally. They fear their own responses in particular, as they do death in general. It is a terrible self-confrontation, and most people don't really know how to handle it safely or even comfortably. Because we have been taught by convention to avoid talking or thinking about death, we fear it blindly. As a result, there are many who cannot be present for a viewing. Yet they are emotionally torn by the need to be with the body, even for a short while. Too often they suffer a heavy sense of guilt for not having been able to be there for the pet.

We understand, intellectually, that death comes to all things. But our conditioned avoidance of this ultimate reality gives us some excuse, up to a point, for denial and bargaining. When faced with death, however, we discover that we know a lot more about it than we had realized. That knowledge also scares some people.

Denial is expressed in unlimited ways, and several studies have been made of it. There are very many varieties of this normal but temporary psychological reaction. Actually, some expression of denial is one of the most common defense mechanisms observed in bereavement. We all feel it, even if slightly or momentarily.

Generally, the best way to respond to denial in others is to accept it until they are ready to face reality on their own—unless there is psychological risk involved. If they feel pushed, or if the denial is criticized too harshly or suddenly, there is a chance of intensifying other underlying psychological problems. A defense mechanism is justifiable, even valuable, when it serves as a temporary "Band-Aid" for protection from immediate and overwhelming problems. But it should not last too long, only sufficient time to allow reality and natural healing to set in. If the response is excessive or prolonged, then the problem should be addressed by a trained professional.

Defense mechanisms are created by the human mind when it needs to hide from some very painful reality. Acceptance of the full truth in one's bereavement is extremely difficult and is accompanied by suffering. It will take some people much longer than others to go through this stage. We must be tolerant and patient during this especially difficult time. Denial will gradually modify into other less destructive expressions and eventually fade away.

Case History

A retired widow in her late fifties was referred because of her acute denial concerning the death of her beloved dog. She had suffered an intense bereavement for her husband, about five years before, and had found much comfort in the dog's loving presence. The relationship between the woman and her eleven-year-old pet had always been close, but it became very dependent, as well. She doted on the dog to the point that her close friends felt it was becoming a spoiled brat. The situation became so obvious and obnoxious that she was criticized by nearly everyone. Her response was to escape into a lonely life without company. She rarely saw people any longer and secluded herself and her adored dog from the world.

Then, inevitably, the pet died. There was nothing the veterinarian could do to prevent it. The dog was about sixteen years old, and its heart just gave out in its sleep. Although she was fortunate that her dog died peacefully, the personal tragedy overwhelmed her.

After an elaborate funeral and burial, she decorated her apartment with every possible reminder of her beloved pet. Pictures and toys were prominently displayed, with black and purple crepe placed everywhere to declare her bereavement. Very few friends and family visited her at first. About three days into this bereavement, she started praying fervently for the dog's return to her. Every possible fantasy was utilized, and she lived in the belief that a "simple miracle" would happen, that reality would somehow be reversed for her. Everything was put on "hold" as she waited for the pet's return. Nothing could dissuade her from this passion.

Friends and family tried to show her the error of her thinking. This only made the situation worse, and she refused to let them into the apartment any longer. Fortunately, a friend she still listened to was able to persuade her to seek professional help to ease her terrible grief.

We worked on her unresolved bereavement for her husband and her great fear of death. It was important not to stress her irrational feelings of denial, though. In time she began to accept the painful reality, and the denial ceased—slowly at first. Most of the unavoidable visual reminders of her pet were removed from the apartment, with only a small, shrinelike area remaining. After about six months of psychotherapy she was ready to start her life over again. She has begun to socialize again with family and friends and her entire life has been reconstructed. The prognosis now is very good.

CHAPTER 7

Guilt

*All of the animals except man know that the
principal business of life is to enjoy it.*

—*Samuel Butler*

uilt is a psychological construct based on insecurity or a negative self-evaluation. It is a normal response to failing some
duty or obligation. It differs from disappointment in that guilt
creates an atmosphere of self-blame and punishment. It is closely
related to the emotion of shame, based on some negative incident
that could have been prevented. This is one of the most commonly
experienced responses in the human emotional repertoire.

Interestingly, guilt is not limited to people, although it is a human
invention. We can see it when training or scolding our pets for violating what they already understood to be an expected behavior. An
animal, however, would not feel guilt on its own. That is an emotional response that we have imposed, with our unending list of rules
and regulations. Not surprisingly, in the wild, guilt has not been
observed.

GUILT AND BEREAVEMENT

Here we are particularly interested in the feelings of guilt and
failed obligation that crop up during intense bereavement for a pet.
Whenever we accept the responsibility of a companion animal, we

The unloved are loved.

Courtesy, Hartsdale Canine Cemetery, Inc.

In memory of a beloved horse.

Courtesy, Abbey Glen Pet Memorial Park

willingly take on a moral presumption of absolute reliability. This sense of duty concerns every possible aspect of the pet's life, health, happiness and well-being. It becomes a powerful self-obligation that may well suffer from a lack of perspective. Unfortunately, such a driving attitude can create a vicious cycle that has no way to end. There usually is no place for death in our loving scheme of things. It scares and mystifies us, so we routinely avoid thinking about it whenever we can. When death eventually does come, the shock can easily be distorted into a strong sense of personal inadequacy and guilt. In effect, our emotions tell us we have failed in some way to perform as well as we should have. It makes us feel as if we are responsible for letting the pet die.

We are completely responsible for the pet's nutrition, medicines, medical care, toys, playmates, sexual status and quality of life. The bonding that results is two-way, with the human becoming emotionally dependent on the pet, as well. During the intense emotions of bereavement, we tend to create a powerful sense of guilt. We feel that we have failed to be in total control. We were unable to be perfect in completely protecting the pet from all possible dangers—especially death. In a sense, we assume godlike roles to our pets, but we are still fallible. Our loving protection still cannot control the universe.

RELINQUISHING CONTROL

Responsibility is not solely measured by action or inaction. It is defined by a vast complexity of circumstances that may be beyond our control or comprehension. Despite that reality, we respond with our emotions as if we should have somehow been able to alter or even prevent the contributing factors in the pet's death. We feel a terrible guilt in losing this control.

Generally, during the early stages of mourning, powerful anger, grief and guilt can overwhelm us. These feelings easily distort most attempts at objective thinking. Such irrational pain can be the result of becoming obsessed with what "might have been," had we only done something that easily could have prevented some aspect of the tragedy. We are filled with feelings of remiss, and we ponder over how this fate could have been avoided "if only" we had done something else. It seems as if this kind of guilty thinking loads our minds to the point of bursting. We begin to feel as if we had not been sufficiently responsible to the pet.

We are human, so we long for what we cannot comprehend, and we criticize ourselves unmercifully. But we need to remember that what was done for those circumstances was right, however sad the result. Some counselors refer to this as the "Should've-Could've-If Only" stage. We have all experienced at least some small degree of this expression of guilt and remorse.

Death has always been a mystery, and despite all our impassioned senses of guilt and responsibility, it will always remain elusive. Western civilization treats death as though it is an evil thing, an enemy to be feared and avoided. But that is very foolish, indeed. Since we cannot blame death for the loss, we tend to blame ourselves or others. We seem to act as if death results from a loss of control on our part. We had complete responsibility and it was taken away. Oddly enough, by assigning blame, even to ourselves, we are unconsciously able to regain a tiny sense of control.

Actually, that control never existed. Intellectually this doesn't make much sense, but emotionally it makes all the difference. Maybe you could have done things differently, but isn't that true about everything? This kind of false logic is really an exercise in negative fantasy. Its unexpressed purpose is to give us an excuse to blame or punish ourselves in our anguish. Guilty feelings are tangible, and they offer something we can grasp and feel when trying to prevail over death. They can give us a false sense of security and a feeling of control at this time. Yet things are truly out of control. Maybe it is time for a reality check.

Case History

There was the case of a woman who had her cat declawed after it destroyed furniture and scratched her badly. This seemed the most sensible thing to do at the time. It made life bearable with an otherwise angry and destructive pet. The owner was a person of great responsibility, and she had a deep affection for the cat, despite its bad behavior. It was well understood that without declawing she would have had to give the cat up. However, this logic later gave way to irrational feelings.

About two years later, the cat died from feline leukemia. The woman shifted her chaotic, bewildering grief into feelings of guilt. Somehow, she began to blame herself for making the little remaining time in her pet's life less than it could have been because she interfered. She was convinced that she was guilty of making a bad decision to declaw the cat.

Therapy had to show her that the logic was as faulty as the emotion behind it was intense. As expected, it turned out that there were earlier emotional traumas in her life that had set her up to feel that she was a failure and would always remain one. She was able to identify this feeling as one she had had since childhood—that she deserved to be punished, but didn't know what for. This made her a prime candidate for inventing all sorts of guilt and self-punishment for anything she had been involved with throughout her unhappy life. She soon saw that the death of her cat was only the spark. It ignited a powder keg of underlying re-pressed emotions and feelings that she desperately needed to work on.

While one is experiencing grief, rational thinking sometimes gets sacrificed. As shown, sometimes feelings of guilt can be completely unfounded. It often expresses a neurotic need to perceive one's self as a failure. Deep down, some individuals even feel that any kind of guilt and pain are part of a deserved self-punishment for who or what they are. A perpetual sense of guilt becomes a way of life for these people.

Some individuals go so far in this as to blame it all on the misunderstood concept of original sin. If man is inherently sinful, then it explains and even seems to condone feeling guilty about everything. They sometimes seem to find shelter in this diminishment of the self. Unfortunately, some use this as justification for self-denial, mediocrity or even failure. When a beloved pet dies, these people are the most prone to suffer exaggerated and prolonged guilt.

Death is sensed as a loss of the control you felt when you had complete responsibility for the beloved. If an individual cannot fully accept the personal blame (and nobody can), then he or she may need to pass it on. It is easy to assign fault at this time of emotional distraction. This shifts the self-anger to someone else. This is a variation of one of the most common human inclinations: passing the buck.

Turn-of-the-century memorial.   *Courtesy, Bide-A-Wee 1992, photo by George Wirt*

AFTER THOUGHT

Guilt can also be a product of afterthought. It is more easily creat-ed in the mind of one who is already suffering and vulnerable. This serves no other real purpose but to hurt the one who invents this guilt. The real question each individual should ask is, "Why do I *need* to feel guilty?" It is normal to wonder about responsibility and possi-ble alternatives that we might have taken, but it is very unhealthy to feed a mind-set of contrition. Mistakes can be made, but that is the way humans operate. Nobody is perfect or exempt from this, espe-cially when trying to be faultless for our beloved pets.

Guilt is often a warping of afterthought and reflection. Pet be-reavement frequently is beset with such dilemmas. These uncertain-ties often concern euthanasia or unresolved thoughts about what we might have done better had we only acted differently. If only we had second sight! But we do not. We are human and imperfect, blessed with love and a sense of the ideal. Each expression of guilt needs to be examined separately to determine the reason it was created. The greater the love for a pet, the greater the possibility that feelings of guilt will later find a way of expressing themselves.

But death has slammed the door of life in our face before we could grasp its full significance. When we try to comprehend this shock, so many new problems and questions seem to arise. It is emotionally overwhelming, and at this time we are especially vulnerable to feel-ings of blame and guilt.

Anger can be directed at religion for not being able or willing to help at this terrible time. The few attempted explanations of either death or God don't really give the answers needed now, in this grief. Unfortunately, there are precious few clergy in most Western religions who would even try to help in pet bereavement (see Chapter 15). Do our beloved pets have souls? Is there a heaven for pets? Will we ever see them again? We are flooded with feelings and questions about why such an innocent, good, trusting, loving animal must die. Without an afterlife it just doesn't seem fair; it doesn't make sense.

It is easy to believe that most pets are better than many humans. They are living examples of authentic love, loyalty, innocence and trust. The many evils of humanity do not corrupt the purity of their spirit. So, why doesn't organized religion offer us help in understand-ing the souls of animals? It seems very reasonable that pets should have the promise of some heaven, too. Does that same place include us? Do we rejoin after death? Why can't anyone understand these things? Where does the bereft heart turn? To whom? To what? In trying to better understand our sense of failed responsibility, we need time and support from others who are sensitive to our needs and responses.

Ultimately, however, we have to find that final measure of strength within ourselves. Yes, we lose our perspective when there is death, but we do have some redeeming graces. Our pets loved us despite all our frailties. What was the good they sensed in us? It must have been real then. It must still be real. That beautiful realization should help wash away some of the stubborn guilt that clings to us. Guilt soils the beauty of the memory and should be removed.

RESPONSIBILITY TO OURSELVES

Responsibility must now be shifted to one's self. Be the wonderful person that your pet saw in you. Let yourself grieve constructively by accepting the passing and preserving the loving memories. This is your duty now. If your pet could send you a message, it would tell you to take better care of yourself, since he or she is not there any longer to protect you. Think about that.

Your life and energy are being wasted feeling guilty. Too often this is misplaced and negative energy. Guilt is a normal, deeply personal, human response to having committed some perceived offense. But we are not blameworthy because we are imperfect. Since we are human, we also make mistakes. If they are not viciously intended, don't we deserve forgiveness and some compassion as well? Certainly! But it has to come from within one's self.

Case History

The problems of another patient can illustrate this type of grief. Here we have the case of a young woman in her late thirties who lovingly housed two stray kittens until she could find a home for them. This gave her great pleasure and took about two weeks to accomplish. But her real pet, an older cat, felt jealous during this period.

A few months later, this older pet suddenly came down with a previously undiagnosed congestive heart problem. The pet died just three weeks later, despite every possible attempt at medical assistance.

The young woman could not overcome her grief. She felt guilty about not showing "enough love" to her cat when it must have been feeling jealous. She began to recall how her pet misbehaved and was punished when the kittens were being temporarily housed and cared for. She felt that this surely must have deteriorated her pet's quality of life, somehow contributing to the heart disease and early death. She felt this, but she did not really believe it. She was vulnerable, and a deep sense of personal guilt had free rein over her. Fortunately, she sought professional counseling and soon was shown how to help herself out of this terrible state of mind. She still grieved her loss, but without the guilt.

LEARNING TO FORGIVE

The potential for inventing guilt is vast, and the human mind does some powerful damage to itself at times. Where does one realistically draw the line on responsibility and its fulfillment? Both we and our beloved pets stray a bit from perfection, and this should be realized and accepted. That amazing, loving bond between a human and pet is so special that any transgression is quickly forgiven. It is absolved by our love. But we must punish our pets at times, just as we do our children. This is the way they sometimes must be shown how to behave. Isn't a well-trained, well-behaved pet a happier one? Unquestionably, the training process is necessary, with all its occasional upsets and losses of patience. During bereavement, some people regress back to the training period and seek justification for their guilt. Even something as necessary and benign as kind punishment is used to justify their attitude. They need to feel guilty.

In the role as steward of a pet, we have assumed such total responsibility that we are psychologically unprepared for the sudden release of that duty without our consent. After a lifetime of self-accountability, we still feel responsible, and the feeling does not go away with the pet's death. The patterns we have established over such a long period of time keep us emotionally bonded to them. Since all decisions had been up to us, it is normal to feel that there may have been other things we could have done. This easily develops into a deep, personal sense of guilt that we might have done something else to avert this death.

An emotional conflict with reality can create upsetting moods of self-anger. As already discussed, we can become obsessed, pondering whether destiny is preventable and if we might have intervened. But how much control do we really have over our fates? Some philosophers claim that everything that happens is natural and had to happen exactly as it did.

Even carelessness, as avoidable as it is, should be seen in this light. There are accounts of all kinds, such as that of the puppy on an outdoor tether who was attacked by a possibly rabid, stronger animal. There was a sweet kitten who was carried off by a hawk in front of the horrified pet's owner. One of the most bizarre of these events happened when a man's dog accompanied him fishing at a pond just outside his home in Florida. An alligator seemed to appear out of nowhere. It sneaked up and seized the dog in those terrible jaws, dragging the startled pet into and under the water, while the man shouted and watched helplessly. Another woman discovered, in shock and horror, that she had backed her car over her beloved dog, fatally injuring her pet. There are so many kinds of accidents that happen to our pets. All of these awful events resulted in terrible feelings of guilt for the owners. Each one felt he or she could have prevented the death by being more diligent. They all believed their failed responsibility caused the deaths. They condemned and severely punished themselves with guilt.

Yes, they were guilty. But how long should they have to suffer such heartbreak? When should it ease or stop? How can they ever give themselves forgiveness? Accidents will happen, but we cannot be on guard all the time, and we are not all-knowing, either. Death can even be caused by the normal use of anesthetic during a routine operation. Indeed, there are risks we haven't even thought about. It is impossible to prevent all accidents. All we can do is try to improve the odds of survival. We live with danger all the time. A normal street crossing is a potential hazard. One could even be killed by a piece of falling meteorite. Who can say there should have been preventive action?

Somehow, we have to reach deep within ourselves and come up with the saving grace of self-love. We must be able to forgive ourselves and ease up on the guilt. The terrible memory will be with us always—but so will the love and wonderful memories. If the pet were to sit in judgment over you, surely there would be forgiveness.

Guilty feelings are an invented response to accepting responsibility that we are not able to uphold. We each have such varied and unique complexities of personality that no generalization will ever satisfy all. It is hoped that by examining each example in this perspective, we can more effectively help ourselves deal with this problem at this particularly grievous time in our lives.

Pet lovers have very good hearts and generous spirits. Without hesitation, we generously give all for our beloved companions. Isn't that exactly what they would want us to do for ourselves, during this time of bereavement?

"Sleeping" and at one with nature. *Courtesy, Hartsdale Canine Cemetery, Inc.*

Memorial to the adored pets of Vern and Irene Castle.
Courtesy, Hartsdale Canine Cemetery, Inc.

CHAPTER 8

Depression

There is no greater sorrow than to recall
a time of happiness in misery.

—Dante

Doctors speak of diseases in terms of their mortality and morbidity. The mortality of a condition is a reference to its ability to end life, whereas morbidity measures a condition's degree of misery and pain. Today, a strong case of the flu has a very low mortality index, but its morbidity is quite high. The same can be said of the depression aspect of the mourning process. Fortunately for many, it can be brief, as well as mild.

It should be pointed out that many people in deep bereavement experience feelings of depression throughout the entire mourning process. Its intensity always diminishes with time, however, which eases the dominating tone of sadness and bittersweet memory. Even though it is sometimes identified as one of the stages of grieving, depression may crop up at any time, not necessarily in the order listed.

At this phase, our emotional strength seems to give out, and things may feel as if they are crushing down on us. We just need to detach ourselves from them for a while. All we seem to care about is the pet's death and our own misery. A sense of numbness and indifference creeps over everything else, and we don't seem to care. Life feels overwhelming and very sad.

SYMPTOMS OF DEPRESSION

Psychologists classify depression as a syndrome characterized by several different symptoms, such as a markedly lowered mood, difficulty in thinking and unusual physical fatigue. There may be signs of anxiety, obsessive thought, appetite loss and difficulty with normal sleep patterns. All of this is dominated by an overwhelming attitude of gloom, dejection and despair. Things do not seem to matter much, and those suffering may feel ambivalent about nearly everything. Generally, they prefer to be alone to stew in the juices of their misery. There is an old adage that says, "Misery loves company." Generally, that does not hold true for depressed people. They prefer their suffering in silence.

Depression can develop to any degree of intensity, but it is not a cause of alarm unless it seems to pose a danger to the individual. Generally, that could be predicted by one's emotional health prior to the tragedy. Also in this state, the mind temporarily dulls things that can cause it grief. This offers a necessary escape from some of the intensity for a while.

FEELING SELF-DESTRUCTIVE

Suicidal feelings are much more common than is generally believed. Fortunately, suicide is most often contemplated and not attempted. Severe depression poses a more serious potential danger, though. Repeated or dangerous self-destructive thoughts are not unheard of during bereavement for a pet. Such behavior should always be counseled by a qualified practitioner of mental health. There is no stigma or shame in it. However, normal depression is usually a relatively minor phase, despite the intense degree of emotional torment involved. It will usually pass in a few days or so.

Only a tiny percentage of depressed mourners entertain serious considerations about suicide. These individuals almost always have well-defined, long histories of emotional upset and disturbance. The grief of bereavement is only the trigger mechanism for these thoughts, not a cause. Those people may be at risk at such a time. Normally, this is nothing to worry about during the typical depression that is related to mourning.

It can be said that depression is probably the most normal of all responses to the death of a pet. But we become upset in differing degrees at the loss of anything we hold dear. This includes our habits and patterns of behavior, as well as our possessions. Even the owner of a dented car, a torn jacket or a broken toy can become depressed. Certainly the death of a beloved pet is a more than sufficient cause for depression. It is a very normal human reaction.

WITHDRAWAL

During this aspect of mourning, we tend to withdraw from the rest of the world. People and incidents don't affect us as they normally would. We may become disconsolate and listless, concerned only with the pet we have lost and the misery we are drowning in. Not only do we not feel good about anything, we don't want to feel better. Our sense of self-worth is at its lowest, and we really don't seem to care much about anything.

This condition dulls even our powerful guilt responses, as well as pangs of conscience and shock. We become quiet, dull, listless, melancholy and ambivalent about things in general. Nothing seems to motivate depressed mourners as they withdraw into themselves. Fortunately, this improves with time. Normally, depression should not last more than a few days to a week. If it persists, with little or no sign of improvement, then professional help is suggested.

At this time it seems as if there is nothing left in the world to ever smile about again. We are in a retreating, self-protective state of mind during this stage. Our sorrow for ourselves and our pets acts like a barrier between us and the rest of the world. It can seem as if it takes all of our best efforts to just endure. Even gentle, caring friends who want to help may seem pushy and invasive to the depressed person who needs more time to be alone and cry. We may feel at this time that feelings for the deceased pet are too personal and intense to even try to share with anyone else. We need some time and privacy to recover from our depression. We constantly hear about time being one of the best healers. Although that can seem meaningless or even cavalier to anyone in deep mourning, it always seems to be true.

During this phase, we may even seem to "lose" ourselves for a while. We are involved in a total and disproportionate focus on the beloved deceased companion. Also, we may be distraught because religious and philosophical teachings don't assure us of an afterlife for this pet, and we are unsure whether we will ever meet again after death. It can be additionally depressing because there are no answers when we need them most. We may feel at this time that life has little or no value. The future seems to have no meaning or importance. These are normal symptoms of depression, and they will pass.

A HEALING STAGE

Mourners need communication with others, loving consideration and time to be alone. Only in cases of abnormal depression will those in bereavement be unable to take even some small action to help themselves. Most of us will pass quickly enough through this seemingly unending but healing phase. It helps greatly to be able to talk out our story with some sympathetic person or persons. Close friends and support groups are probably the best help during this, the saddest phase of the mourning process.

Surprisingly, depression as a stage in bereavement does serve a good purpose. It diminishes the intensity of emotions and gives us time to live with and assimilate the grim, new reality. We meditate on the pet's death and begin to develop a new spiritual strength and perspective that we could not have had before. It is all part of the amazing healing process that nature has provided for us.

When the depression passes, we are much closer than before to the resolution stage of the mourning. Things are beginning to look upward now. The worst part is over. For the first time since the death, it is possible to sense the easing of pain and to see some light at the end of the tunnel.

Case History

An attractive, single woman in her late thirties had a history of being lonely and moderately forlorn. She owned a large, two-year-old male dog on whom she relied as her protector and closest companion. There was strong therapeutic value in this, but it was compromised by her becoming somewhat reclusive and giving up on marriage or ever finding a suitable boyfriend. She lived with her beloved dog in a sort of emotional cocoon, isolated from everyone else.

The young dog died quite suddenly and unexpectedly from a respiratory ailment with cardiac complications. Almost immediately, the woman went into shock and deep depression. She felt panicky, abandoned, mildly suicidal and completely alone. Her job performance suffered, and the rest of her time was spent crying alone at home. She believed that nothing could ever make her smile again, and she said she wanted to die. Fortunately, her alert and compassionate neighbor noted some of these danger signs and finally persuaded her to come for counseling.

After a few sessions of sharing her heartache and utter dejection, we were able to plan some constructive direction in her thinking. Focus was placed on her family and friendly relationships. After getting into serious therapy and analysis of her more formative years, she was able to get some insight into many of the disappointments and problems she had experienced as a child and why she was always so emotionally insecure and lonely. That insight helped her come out of the clinical depression that her dog's death had triggered.

Her history revealed many years of low self-esteem and weak ego strength. She had always felt somewhat inferior and alone. Her alcoholic father was deceased, and her elderly mother, with whom she never had a close relationship, lived halfway across the country. Her only sibling, a brother, abused her as a child and had been estranged from her for many years.

In a few sessions, her bereavement was able to progress to a reasonable resolution. Then we were able to go on in detail to analyze her underlying feelings of inadequacy. She became aware of the powerful symbolism her dog had and her reasons for shyness and low self-esteem.

She is in long-term therapy, but is now leading a happier and much more active life. She is still a bit defensive and laughs about her "pet rock" that needs no sustenance or care and can't die. Frequent, short travel vacations have begun to help give her a new base to improve her ego strength. Her social life is much improved and is growing even healthier. Now her dream is to meet a good man, settle down and raise a small family, with a dog. The prognosis is excellent, as constructive therapy continues.

DEDICATED
TO THE MEMORY OF
THE WAR DOG
ERECTED BY PUBLIC CONTRIBUTION
BY DOG LOVERS, TO MAN'S MOST
FAITHFUL FRIEND, FOR THE VALIANT
SERVICES RENDERED IN THE
WORLD WAR
1914 — 1918

Dedicated to the memory of the unknown canine soldier.

Courtesy, Hartsdale Canine Cemetery, Inc.

CHAPTER 9

Resolution (Closure)

Our deeds still travel with us from afar.
And what we have been makes us what we are.

—George Eliot (Mary Ann Evans)

T here is a time to have and to hold, and a time to let go. We will know joy just as we must know sorrow. This final phase of mourning is a time of spiritual inner healing. It is finally the time when we can release the pain without diminishing the beloved memory. Closure is the knitting up of open wounds, but there will always be a secret scar. It is the taking of a brave step forward, putting things into new harmony. This is finally the time for letting go. That means allowing the focus of emotion and attention to shift, permitting each of us to continue with our own life's growth. This is when the pain changes from an immobilizing force to precious remembrance, hope and self-regeneration. This is the time for closure.

Finally, the time has come to stop clutching teary memories and learn to incorporate them as loving components of our new lives. Our lives go on, but we never let go of the love that is still so cherished. It becomes a part of us, a fundamental passion, never to be lost. What we do with that and how we may choose to memorialize the loss will vary with each individual.

Completing the passage through the bereavement process will in no way degrade one's intensely personal love for a deceased pet. This is the part of each mourner's life when functioning must be resumed. At this point of transition, each of us has become different from before. Now, left without the pet's physical presence, we are enriched with a new dimension of its love. And that is very healing. In reaching closure, we learn to incorporate that loving memory into the wiser and better person we have become because of this. The love and memories live on and forever enrich us.

A DIFFICULT CONCEPT

Death is the inevitable and only destination of every life. It is that simple. We so easily accept the concept of birth and living, but we become upset and troubled by thinking about the end of life. Because it is so completely mysterious to us, this subject becomes too disturbing to confront when not absolutely necessary. Most of our experiences with the ending of life are rationalized or blocked out. We try to pretend it away, and we try to deny that death is always around the corner, in every life. We like to make-believe that it can be controlled by modern medicine, when it may be only postponed, at best. And sometimes that is not for the best.

But right now, during the mourning process, we are obsessed with a sense of anguish and personal tragedy, and we feel helpless. We are ever so unprepared for death. Even the word "death" provokes general discomfort. As a natural result, we have created many word substitutes and euphemisms. We even think in euphemistic ways, avoiding direct confrontation with the subject. People don't generally discuss this topic. It is usually extremely uncomfortable to even hear others talk about this topic. Thus, we are always unready and frightened, as well as completely overwhelmed by the grim finality, when it comes.

CHANGING ATTITUDES

Western culture needs to make some adjustments to its attitude toward death. Fortunately, it is beginning to show some changes. The introduction of Eastern philosophy has enlightened large numbers of seekers in many ways. As we work our way toward improving knowledge, we begin to realize that death is neither bad nor the enemy. It is a natural part of the life sequence. We have been acculturated to be terrorized by the idea of life's end and the fear that there may be nothing else afterward. Since we celebrate a birth as a beginning of an unknown life, we should celebrate death as the logical end to a beautiful life that gave us a very special love. The funeral and mourning should incorporate the sadness and loss, while also commemorating and honoring that life. If nothing but tears and grief are there, then something very important has been left out.

It is interesting to note that "primitive" or underdeveloped civilizations accept death much more easily and rationally than we do. That is not because they are less sensitive or intelligent. Simply, they have not yet been deceived into believing that nature can be controlled so completely. All of civilization's powers cannot revoke death. All the scientific and technological command and dominion that we have attained over other things is useless here. We cannot continue to pretend that death does not follow naturally. If we close our eyes, it doesn't go away. This is like the image of an ostrich hiding its head in a hole in the ground to avoid danger. Time and death will always catch up with us, even if we try to ignore the fact. Death should not be characterized as something arcane, supernatural or bad. All living things must die. Unfortunately, we have come to feel that we have gained such mastery and control over life and illness that death is a mistake, or an accident, and can be constrained. But it is a natural event, and it will go on forever.

We love cut flowers and enjoy their beauty. But when they wilt and die, it is time to put them aside. There is no sadness in that. The life of a beloved pet, or *anything* else, is really very similar. We are enriched and deeply affected by the years of the pet's love and companionship. But this profound relationship has reached down to the core of our existence and helped change our sense of identity. Although it is hard to put aside the physical being, we keep the love and joy within us. We have to learn to accept that there is a natural limit to each lifetime. If an individual can add religious significance and consolation to this outlook, all the better. To see only sad things in a death is to lose perspective and fail in our respect. It diminishes the value of that life. That is not the way we want it.

We are learning that even stars and galaxies are born and die, in turn. Somehow, in the grand scheme of all things, everything is related. All of the ancient stars that have exploded have created newer elements that spread out to help form even newer stars and galaxies.

And these in turn have done the same, all the way down the line for sixteen billion years, creating us and all the present physical matter in our cosmos of today. Actually, we are made of stardust—everything is. The constant cycle of life and death is the rule of all things. Everything in nature has a beginning and an end. It is unnatural to see death as the enemy to be feared and hated. Somehow, we have to develop a healthier and broader outlook on the meanings and values of life. That is why the wisdom of the East still has so much to teach us. We are all part of nature, and we need to develop a more natural outlook on all things, especially our own lives.

Mourning for a pet has always been kept very private and secret, as a means of self-protection from unqualified criticism. We have reached a point in our cultural evolution where this humane expression is finally being let out from under wraps. People are beginning to talk more freely about the effect of a pet's death upon them. Our personal vulnerability and stigmas of shame are being reduced or removed. So many people are being made aware of the vast numbers of us who have experienced this type of grief. We are no longer looked upon as social oddities. There is some encouragement in this realization, which encourages us to no longer feel as restricted in expressing our heartfelt feelings and emotions for a pet's death.

A STEP-BY-STEP PROCESS

The entire mourning process is a living-through situation in which we are unconsciously preparing ourselves, step-by-step, to let go of what we hold so dear. The very term "letting go" can be misleading. It does not mean that we forget the beloved or stop having loving memories. Closure only comes to us gradually, with the acceptance of the grim reality and its effects. It is achieved when thoughts of a beloved pet no longer occupy the forefront of our minds. It permits us to remember and feel all the love, without the shock and grief caused by a pet's death. When we are able to reach a sense of closure, we can pick up and go on with *our own* lives. During the early stages of bereavement, this may seem selfish. At that point we may still feel an irrational need to suffer. It may seem to us that if we stopped hurting, we would stop loving. And that thought is intolerable. But later, we will finally see that it is not true. That special love has transformed itself into a permanent part of one's new self.

To help reach a sense of closure, the following time-tested method is suggested:

> **Make a list**—Itemize particular times and situations that still give you special pain and trouble in your bereavement. Continue expanding this list over several days. Later, read it over and look for some common denominators. What repeated themes are there? To help put this into better perspective, it is best to discuss your list and themes with someone you trust and respect.

> **Don't berate yourself for not feeling as much pain as you first did**—Sometimes we tend to be anxious about what may feel like too rapid or even too slow a recovery. The healing process makes us stronger and better, but it involves pain, time, self-respect and it takes lots of patience.

WHAT WE LEARN

It is often said that time heals all wounds. Superficially, this statement is correct. But it is trite and incomplete. A better statement would explain that what really heals is learning to live with wounds. That requires time to achieve and complete. but time can dull recollections; that is not what we seek here. What we want is a beautiful memory, filled with loving sentiments that live on in us. That is the best memorial possible.

With the passage of time, we don't ever lose that special love for a beloved life that has ended. However, we do learn to be less and less overwhelmed by the death. We learn to let go of the shock and pain, but not the cherished loving memories and associations. And we go on living, with this refinement in us. Unfortunately, part of life is suffering, and we have to learn this the hard way. There is no choice.

The process of gradually picking ourselves up to continue with our lives is upsetting, yet necessary. But, somehow, this is accomplished in time. Mostly, the hard part is done at the subconscious level of awareness and healing. Gradually, the shock diminishes, and we are able to go on.

There are some who even respond as if they have become different people. Indeed, they have changed. Others may feel a spiritual dedication to the pet's living memory and redirect their lives accordingly. We move on and step up on the staircase of experience, ever changing and improving as we go. With each step we are more aware, and hopefully wiser. The experience of living with a beloved pet has been an enriching one, one that benefits us forever. It adds a special endearing memory and strength to us, now and for the rest of *our* lives.

We become products of our former experiences. After discovering the beauty and wonder of that special loving life, we owe it to that living memory to heal and grow ourselves. We must go on. Certainly, that is what your pet would want for you, if you were to be able to put its feelings into human thought. Consider that.

At this state of resolution and closure, it is heartwarming to be able to think that your new life alone, without the deceased pet, can become a living memorial. Your improved outlook can be the ultimate testimony to that love.

CHAPTER 10

Other Kinds of Loss

That grim abduction still eluded me, until too late,
with pitiless events in nature's normalcy called fate.
Dispossessing profanation, so irrevocable,
wrests my unremitting grief to wretchedness and wait.

—*Modern Rubaiyat, Wallace Sife*

M ost people think about the loss of a pet in terms concerning its death. But there is another kind of loss that we should all be made aware of because it can happen to nearly any one of us. This other horrible experience is bereavement for a pet resulting from its disappearance. One hears of all sorts of shocked and grieving owners, advertising desperately for the return of their beloved companion animals. Sometimes very large rewards are offered, even by poor families, just to bring that cherished pet back. There is no measure of an adored pet, other than the love we have for it when it is with us and the grief we suffer when it is gone.

Many pet owners find it necessary to seek bereavement counseling when their animals disappear. Some of these pets probably strayed away and confronted the perils of traffic, predators, vicious dogs and God knows what else. Their owners are in all stages of mourning, despite the fact that there was no direct relationship with death. Many seem to be even worse off than my patients who have recently deceased pets. These people are in a unique category of bereavement because they can still cling to a golden spark of hope that their beloved animals are still alive and may yet return home. But they know that the probability drops to near zero as time passes. Sadly, for the following few months and years, they may never know that the pet is dead. If they at least knew that, then the worry would be over, which might ease some of the terrible grief. Now, however, the awful grip of uncertainty, guilt and suspense dominates every waking moment—and even their dreams.

WHEN A PET DISAPPEARS

There are so many ways a pet can disappear. A bird, even with clipped flight feathers, may flutter out a just-opened door or a window opened only a crack. Dogs and cats stray and get lost. They can be picked up by people who keep them as their new pets, or they may become members of feral groups, living on garbage and anything else they can get. There are dangers such as vicious feral animals that are natural predators in some parts of the country and contemptible humans who delight in trying to drive over any animal they see alone on the road. Many strays are captured by animal control officers and sent off to be euthanized. And then there are the professional suppliers to the experimental labs. These accomplished human predators are always on the prowl for any dog or cat they can find.

Pets are frequently stolen out of yards and cars, and then they are sold to labs for testing and vivisection experiments. It is worse than a jungle out there. There is no animal more vile than an evil human. The unrelenting guilt and grief we go through as we try to live through this open-ended experience is like no other kind of bereavement.

It is natural to experience most of the stages of loss when a pet disappears. But some of these are intensified and distorted by uncertainty and an overwhelming sense of failed responsibility. Unfortunately, there can be no real resolution to the pain. Closure could come with either the return of the pet or certain knowledge of its death. The initial stage of shock is even slightly different. There still may be hope, however dim it is. Usually, there is no response of disbelief because of the urgent circumstances demanding full awareness of the situation. The anger is also a bit different, with most of it directed at oneself for being so negligent. In the case of petnapping, the anger is also directed at the thief and others in general who would deliberately do this to your pet. It becomes a terrible exercise in rage and dire frustration.

There is no such thing as being only a little careless when a pet disappears. It is a matter of all or nothing. Anger quickly turns into guilt. "Should have," "could have" and "if only" fill us with passion. But it is too late. That is when a variation of the denial stage kicks into gear, and fantasy offers some hope. We offer up all sorts of prayers to try to bargain or plead with God for the return of the pet. This phase can be even more painful for an owner when the pet disappears, rather than for one whose pet dies. But sometimes we are very lucky—sometimes lost pets are returned and strays come home.

PREVENTABLE LOSSES

There are so many ways a beloved pet can be taken from us that it is important to consider them—hopefully before they have the opportunity to take place. This kind of loss is often preventable, as contrasted to death, which is inevitable. A very important lesson can be learned in the following pages, and it can help prevent this type of loss from happening to you. Constant watchfulness is required in the care of our pets. That is part of the commitment we make as stewards.

Cats can be very efficient at escaping or getting lost. Everyone hears about cats climbing up trees and then becoming too fearful to come down. Sometimes local fire departments will not come to the rescue, claiming they are too busy at the moment with higher priority disasters. Cases of lost cats have been reported as a result of this kind of situation, when the pet later disappears. Naturally, the owner had expected that the cat would eventually come down, despite its fright. That, however, could take many hours, and most people cannot just wait there for its return. There are also many cases of cats who escaped out of a momentarily opened door or disappeared out a partially opened window.

Dogs are frequently reported missing because of other careless conditions or practices that their owners engaged in. Most of these losses also arise from preventable circumstances. Some dogs are regularly allowed to freely roam their neighborhood. Their owners have many different, inexcusable justifications for permitting this. More often than we would like to admit, these beloved pets disappear and are never seen again. Was it because of thieves who routinely sell them to labs or strangers taking them in as their new pets? Or was there some kind of terrible accident? The bereaving owner will probably never know.

The same missing pet complaint also arises from situations where dogs are routinely tied up outside stores, while their owners are inside, shopping. Again, the excuses and justifications are easy to come by, but the pet is lost. Now it's too late to defend against this! Sadly, there are many recorded instances of concerned people who tried to warn the owners, but who were routinely told to mind their own business. This is another irony of preventable loss.

Stealing a dog from a yard or a car is the most common type of pet-napping. No one ever thinks that such a thing will happen to his or her pet, but it does—and can be deterred so easily. This does not mean that one should confine the dog in a car with the windows shut to prevent criminal opening of the locks. Too many deaths by heat prostration happen every year because of that. A dog left in a car in the sun can die in as little as twelve minutes, or it may be left with permanent brain damage in much less time. The owner must work this problem out before the danger or possible theft has a chance to happen. The professional petnapper is very adept at luring and baiting most animals, in all kinds of situations. Don't rely on your pet being too smart to be fooled.

Some dogs are more frightening than others to neighbors. At times these pets have to be removed by law because of their biting, excessive noise or just because they are of a breed and temperament that some communities fear. Most people who train their dogs for protection or to attack others are just asking for action to be taken against them and their pets (who were innocently turned into "monsters"). When these dogs are taken away, even these selfish owners suffer their private grief. Regardless of who or what we are, we all see and feel things in our own perspectives.

Many landlords and other housing authorities do not allow pets. Tenants who do not know this, or who disregard that clause in their leases, are almost always required to finally give up their beloved pets. In other cases, dog and cat owners have to relocate, and their new landlords forbid pets. Sometimes just the travel conditions can make it impossible to take the pet. And others somehow lose their companion animals while on a trip, and they cannot stop for an indefinite time to search for them. The resulting grief immediately changes their lives, and the emotional scars can last forever. These are also very commonplace occurrences that too often could have been avoided by some careful advance planning.

Loss Due to Divorce

Divorce is another situation that can cause the loss of a pet. As necessary as the break-up of a family may be, both parties always suffer. But somebody has to lose the pet. One partner takes it, along with other agreed upon possessions and goods. The tragedy is compounded when the winning ex-spouse really does not love the pet as much as the other. It is too often used as a means to get back at the other person—and the animal's best interests are traded off with other angry or competitive settlements of property. Whoever loses custody of the pet suffers other feelings of outrage, as well. This kind of loss is always complicated by additional problems that result from the broken marriage and the final unpleasant compromises and settlements. But at least in this kind of loss there is some solace in knowing that the pet is alive and well—not missing. Its basic safety and well-being are most likely not in any danger.

However, in cases of domestic violence, when a woman finally gets up the courage to relocate to a shelter, other problems can complicate matters. Pets are not allowed in such places, and they often have to be left behind with the abusive husband. Such women deeply suffer the loss of their pets, and they also worry that their companion animals may be deliberately mistreated in retaliation. That fear is often well-founded. There have been too many cases recorded in which the brutal man beat, tortured or even killed a pet that was dear to the woman. Sometimes the pet's safety is used as a hostage situation to get her to come back. It is all part of a very sick and abusive way of exercising control.

When a Pet Is Removed

There are also many instances in which pets are forcibly taken from homes by animal control personnel. This is often initiated by complaints of inhumane crowding and inadequate treatment. This is frequently accompanied by all sorts of disagreeable noises and smells. Too often these animal abusers are out of touch with reality, on several different levels. They may well be of limited mental competence, but all too often they are just very foolish and extremely self-indulgent. In their narrow perspective, they love their hordes of animals and don't seem to realize that they are doing them actual harm. These lonely people also go through the painful stages of bereavement for their seized pets. Everyone sees his own problems as no one else can. We all have our private sorrows and wretched reactions in bereavement. As pet lovers and humanists, we must keep our objectivity and awareness that *all* grief should merit some compassion, regardless of the circumstances.

Sickness and disability are other common reasons for having to remove people's pets. When some people no longer have the ability to care for them, the pets must be picked up and sent somewhere. Unfortunately, most often they go off to shelters to be euthanized. These people are very loving, but they are too infirm to continue their responsibilities as stewards of their cherished pets. In addition to an agonizing sense of loss and bereavement, their misfortunes often cause other problems. All this becomes even more complicated by a terrible sense of failure and utter loneliness without their beloved companion animals. As a result, they often suffer further emotional, spiritual and physical collapse. Pets can be our psychological and spiritual life preservers in seas that would quickly drown us.

Occasionally, utility animals, trained to assist people with disabilities, are stolen. Their unfortunate owners, already at such a tremendous disadvantage, then have to grieve about the possible terrible fate of these beloved companion animals. They bond much more powerfully and depend entirely on their animals for even a small sense of independence and self-esteem. The loss of these pets can sometimes be too much to bear, especially for older or extremely handicapped people. One woman who had been confined to a lifetime in a wheelchair died of grief after her trained assistance dog was stolen. She loved her dog dearly, and the bonding had been very intense. For nearly three years that dog had been her dearest friend, and it also personified her strength to go on with her tortured daily existence. The horrors of what might have befallen her adored companion animal were too much to contend with. The unbearable uncertainty and loneliness caused her to suffer a fatal heart attack.

Too often these very highly trained dogs are sold to experimental labs, just as additional bodies, along with surplus anonymous shelter animals and stolen family pets. It has been documented that many labs remove all identification when they buy animals. Cases have been verified in which even ID tattoos were surgically removed or made unreadable. These institutions and the fiends who supply them with animals are some of the vilest elements in our society. They continue to thrive under existing laws that protect and encourage them to continue. They are modern-day vampires. Aside from the horrors inflicted on these pets, the lives of the people who love them are broken and can never be the same. They never know the fate of their lost companions, and the labs are their worst fear. Even death is preferred to this appalling, torturous fate.

We occasionally hear of pet snakes escaping from their confines and disappearing. Sometimes they show up days later in the most unlikely of places, still in their homes. But too often they are just gone, never to be found again. They may all too easily have crawled into hidden spaces and died there. The temperature may have dropped, causing them to lose energy and become fatally entrapped. Most people are surprised that the owners of snakes can get so extremely upset emotionally. The most common response to this kind of loss is that a cold-blooded reptile doesn't show love and affection as other pets do, and it couldn't possibly be as loved as a more common pet is. But this seemingly logical response doesn't hold true. It is based on exactly the same kind of prejudice that we have been fighting all these years in expressing bereavement for dogs and cats. Who is to be anyone else's judge when it comes to loving and feeling grief? The spirit and hope that we want for ourselves in "coming out of the closet" with our own grief in pet bereavement is exactly the same for the owners of less understood or liked species of animals. There can be no exceptions or attitudes of superiority or scorn here. The tendency to give snake and other reptile owners short shrift should send us a shocking message about how close we are to being guilty of what we condemn in other, less sensitive individuals. As pet lovers, we must respect all pets, as well as their owners' feelings of bereavement. This is a matter of simple love, understanding and tolerance. The respect we want is the same that we must give. Sitting in judgment of other people's feelings and grief is the very problem that others have plagued us with. What right has anyone to decide if another person's grief is justified? So if the beloved pet is a lizard or even a goldfish, we *must* respect the feelings. Someone is hurting, which is all that should really matter. We are the animal lovers, and God bless all of us.

PETS FREE TO GOOD HOME

Some desperate families, unable to keep their pets, take out "Free to Good Home" ads. Many of these animals are taken from their homes with false promises of a new, good life. They are then unscrupulously sold by licensed U.S. Department of Agriculture (USDA) "B" dealers to research facilities that pay hundreds of dollars for each healthy, gentle dog or cat. Stolen pets are occasionally recovered from "respectable" research institutions across the nation.

Last Chance For Animals, a nonprofit organization in California, is actively pursuing ways to combat this national abuse, including U.S. Congressional action. Through ambitious, vigorous campaigns, it continues to stop pet theft and the profit it offers some individuals. This is the only organization to ap-prehend, bring to trial, convict and send to prison licensed "B" dealers, who are selling stolen companion animals to experimental laboratories. To help in the mission to eliminate this kind of vile activity, or if you have any information about pet theft in your area, call *Last Chance For Animals* at (800) 271-6096 or (888) 88-ANIMALS.

RESPONSES TO A PET'S DISAPPEARANCE

The loss of a pet is a terrible experience, but perhaps there is nothing worse than loss through disappearance. The responses are different, and as already indicated, the grieving stages are often distorted. The only escape from the haunting, non-closure of this experience is by conscious repression of the feelings and bad memories. Of course, that is not a healthy way to reconcile a problem, but in this exceptional circumstance, it seems to be the only release from endless heartache.

Deliberately repressed feelings always lead to unconsciously suppressed complications. They can fester within us all our lives unless intensive psychotherapy is employed. The bereavement one suffers for a missing pet can be even worse than the grief we go through in responding to its death. This is like an open sore that doesn't really heal. The comparison comes to mind of the emotional reactions of families of combat personnel who are reported "missing in action," with no trace of them ever found. How do their families find closure with this? It is exactly the same.

Truth is often stranger than fiction. The famous American short story author O'Henry often made this claim. Countless daily dramas are being played out in amazing variations on all themes, including the losses of beloved pets. One graphic example of this is illustrated in the unusual and completely unexpected tragic experience of one family.

Case History

A young father of two children was dying of cancer. Shortly before his death he gathered his small family around his hospital bed and told them he wanted them to get a German Shepherd Dog to love, and who could be their protector when he was gone. He dd not discuss this in advance with his wife, and the idea came as quite a surprise. It was something the family had never thought about before, but in the grief of their bereavement, they accepted this as his last wish, which had to be honored.

The young mother got a Shepherd puppy but didn't know the first thing about dogs or their training. She was overwhelmed by her bereavement and had to be all things for her two children at the same time. The frisky pup quickly grew into a large, slightly spoiled, affectionate young dog, and it was loved as their surrogate protector—a symbol of perceived replacement for the deceased father.

The children were not too careful about keeping him on its leash in the yard, and after about a year, the dog disappeared. Then, along with all the usual problems and heartache of losing a pet this way, unexpected additional complications suddenly arose. In addition to their grief for the missing dog, they now suffered an unexpected and renewed bereavement for the father. With the loss of the pet he wanted to represent him by watching over them, he seemed to die again in their hearts. They were completely overwhelmed by this double blow and had to go into intensive family and individual therapy. Despite their eventual healing and recovery, some emotional scars will always be there in each of them

When we lose beloved pets, we always lose secret parts of ourselves, as well. When conditions prevent our ever being able to find closure, healing can never be completed. Although time seems to relieve all wounds, this kind of unresolved grief creates suppressed problems that may continue to disturb us for the rest of our lives. While therapy can treat this quite successfully, nothing short of amnesia can remove the memory of this special kind of loss. So we must do something positive about learning to live with it.

We all have different kinds of personal regrets and feelings of misgivings in our lives, but they belong in the past. Now it is our primary responsibility and duty to ourselves to put aside whatever emotional baggage we are left with and move on. Personal growth must never stop. We owe that to ourselves, as well as to all who love us. And that also must include our beloved lost pets.

Another
Pet?

A friend is a present you give yourself.

—*Robert Louis Stevenson*

There are many people whose personalities are ideal for owning a pet. The relationship they create with their pets is one of great mutual love and trust. In this instance, pet and human lead an enhanced, happy life together in a marvelous, symbiotic relationship. Each partner gives and gets in deeply personal ways that are only beneficial. Such a relationship can be enriching beyond description.

Usually, these people are the ones who are hardest hit emotionally when the pet dies. And there will be a time during the initial bereavement period when even these "naturals" are not yet ready for another pet. It is almost a sure thing, though, that they will want another one, some day. But when? Although this may not be a major problem, sometimes there are circumstances that make this decision very difficult.

ARE YOU READY?

Timing is everything when considering whether to get a new pet. You must be ready for the new relationship, or both you and the new

"Good-bye My Loves."   Courtesy, Hartsdale Canine Cemetery, Inc.

Mariposa and
Rose Marie.
Courtesy, Hartsdale
Canine Cemetery, Inc.

pet may suffer because of your underlying resentment. Usually, we may well be prepared, but we are hesitant or even fearful. This could easily feel like betrayal to the deceased pet, even though it really isn't. Indeed, resentment or even feelings of rejection may follow if the replacement is made too soon. Most people need to be alone for a while with their memories. Remember, children are people, too. If they are not too young, let them in on the underlying thinking and the decision-making process, as well.

A new pet can stimulate a healthy improvement of your lifestyle. But you have to be ready. Another side benefit is that this new pet opens a means to meeting new people. After a period of bereavement and depression, a new start can be very beneficial. We become exposed to social situations when walking a dog, buying pet food in the store, attending membership meetings at a pet club and so on. Regular walks also provide us with well-needed exercise. We get out of the house and break the grip of isolation. However, being forced prematurely into a new pet relationship is another problem, and one that can be very upsetting.

Advice is cheap, easy to get and usually well-intended. But in the emotionally charged subject of resolving your personal bereavement, no one else can really know your feelings about bringing a new pet into your life. Even you may not be sure of your own readiness. Never let anyone try to talk you into getting another pet. The decision has to come from deep within yourself, and the timing has to feel right to you.

Sometimes people who have lost their pets may be more ready emotionally than they had at first realized. The following exercise will help you to make a decision on this issue. It will offer a graphic demonstration of whether you are ready to have a new pet.

1. Visit an animal shelter. Do this just to look around, not to adopt at this time! You must be firm with yourself about this resolve. Temptation may be strong for the moment, and very hard to resist. Hasty, impulsive decisions can be very much regretted later.

2. Write down your feelings after this visit, and read them again at another time. Share them with a trusted friend. What new feelings are you beginning to have now after the visit? Did you retain a strong memory of any of the

animals you saw? Sometimes, being exposed to these needy companion animals, we unconsciously help ourselves break out of the most maudlin part of bereavement. Feeling pity and love for homeless, lovable animals in this kind of situation can stimulate a quicker resolution to our bereavement. It can change our perspectives in a positive way, without pain or argument. And it is not betrayal.

3. We tend to forget the difficulties in rearing a pet. Do you remember how long it takes for a new pet to adjust to its new home? Do you recall how long it took for you to adapt to a new pet, with all the work, frustration, annoyance, anger, time and expense involved? If you are really ready, your experience might well make the training period easier. You will find out soon enough.

Children who want an "immediate replacement" should have it explained to them that there is no such thing. Each animal is unique, especially in personality. A pet is not a toy, and a new one cannot be used as a substitute for the deceased pet. If they are above the age of four or five, children should experience the mourning period first. Don't try to protect them from this because doing so may cause unnoticed emotional damage. Speak with your children to determine their level of comprehension of the pet's death. Work it out with them.

Bereaved pet owners feel that their loving memory represent something that can never be replaced. It becomes a symbolic link to the past and a sense of one's own continuity and personal history. The thought of getting another companion animal at this time may feel like disloyalty. During the earlier stages of bereavement, before closure, it might well be. But later this does change, and the pain eases.

Getting another pet would mean companionship again. It would be glad to be your new friend, as well. It would be "someone" to care for. Being responsible for a dependent animal's life again is a good experience. Death should not scare us away from new life. But keep in mind that any new pet will have its own personality. Although your new relationship with it may turn out to be wonderful, it will be different from before. It has to be. The new relationship cannot be the same.

It is very important to realize that a beloved pet cannot be "replaced." Some mistaken people try this with other animals of the same breed, sex and markings, and it never works out the way they planned. That is just sheer foolishness. Appearance does not make the pet, and it can never substitute for individuality. The very special relationship and bonding that existed with the old pet was so unique that only its loving memory could take its place. There can be no replacement of that.

When I conduct group support sessions, I usually allow my dog to be present. She senses the grief and goes around the circle of be-reavers, stopping to love and be loved by each one in turn for a few minutes. It is amazing and gratifying to see the therapy a little loving animal can give to people in deep mourning for their own pets. She has been hugged, kissed, whispered to and cried over. Almost without exception, I have been told by patients how helpful this exposure was in easing their grief and assisting them to realize their levels of readi-ness for a new pet.

We can touch and caress our pets. This is so good for us for many reasons. Pets decrease loneliness and depression. It has been proven that our general health improves by being and interacting with them. They lower blood pressure, relax our bodies, help improve our resis-tance to disease and give us amusement and other pleasures. It has been clinically proven that they can lengthen the duration of one's life, while improving its quality as well.

Do you have a strong fear of having to go through another pet's death? If so, would you be able to handle such a loss and bereavement again? The answer is probably yes. But you should not opt for bring-ing another pet into your life until you have worked through your pre-sent grief and early phases of mourning. But no one else can tell you when you are ready. If you feel indecisive about getting another pet, don't do it yet! You can be ready only when and if this ambivalence is replaced by more positive feelings about yourself and a new pet-friend. Only you will be able to sense when the time is right. Stay with your "gut feelings." Trust your instincts; they have much truth underlying them.

Don't rush into getting another pet. But sometimes, under extra-ordinary circumstances, quickly getting another one is advisable. This is rare, however, and always has urgent reasons for its justification. On the other hand, some well-intentioned people try to show their love by giving a replacement pet to a bereaved owner. This caring but fool-ish act can create a major problem. In effect, it forces mourners to

Testimony to a dear monkey.

A monoment at
Bide-A-Wee for former
President Nixon's
dog, Checkers.
Photo by George Wirt

accept an immediate substitute (which cannot be done) well before they may have been able to work out their basic grief. Because we love animals, we will feel sorry for the little orphan, reflexively responding to its needs. Giving someone a replacement pet can be especially cruel if done at the wrong time. It really is forcing one's will upon another person who may not yet be ready to make a reasonable commitment. No one can make such a covenant for that person.

THINGS TO KEEP IN MIND

When you finally do decide to open up your life to another companion animal, there are a few things that should be kept in mind. If you like the same breed and color, that's fine, but do not try to remake the new animal into a replica of your deceased pet. This cannot be done. The initial period of adjustment teaches you, as well as the pet, about the other. Make a new relationship and build it on mutual trust, love and respect. This will be your new friend. Get toys that do not remind you of your deceased pet's playthings. Give this new pet a chance to be wonderful, too, on its own merits. It deserves this respect and love.

Some older people feel they should not get another pet, just in case they become too ill or infirm to continue to care for it. They fear developing a strong bond and then becoming unable to live up to the responsibility. They may worry about dying before the pet does, which could become very complicated. It also would traumatize the pet, which would be terrible. If they live alone, that adds to the potential problems.

Instead of getting another companion animal under these conditions, it may be better to visit with friends and neighbors who have a pet. Most often these people would be happy if an older friend enjoyed and played with their pets, within certain limits. Discuss this with them. Perhaps occasional pet sitting or walking their pets may help fill the need to enjoy a companion animal's company. It is like being a grandparent—with all of the pleasure and little of the responsibility.

Sometimes it is an excellent idea to get another pet before the first one dies. It may make good sense to bring home a baby animal friend for the older one, as well as for the owner. If the older animal accepts this (and most will), the quality of its remaining life will be much improved. This will also have great psychological benefits for the owner, who has "someone" who can share the loss of the older pet when the time comes. Also, the owner will not be left alone. There will be another sweet companion animal to love and care for, and buffer the sorrow.

Remember, a new pet will make many mistakes and possibly cause some damage to your property. Perhaps you forgot this. But, in punishing it, you must never vent your possible anger for the previous pet's death—even if innocently provoked by this youngster. This is another loving life and a completely different set of responsibilities for you.

Three very different examples come to mind, examples that illustrate interesting problems concerning getting a new pet.

Case History

An unmarried woman in her mid-fifties was referred for therapy. She held a middle-management position in a large corporation and was financially secure. She came for help because of constant, upsetting dreams about her cat, which had been dead for over a year. It was apparent that she was being tortured by this and needed help.

She was compulsively talkative, and she rambled on about her relationship with the cat. She firmly believed it had shared her company during a previous existence in ancient Egypt. She believed she had been a member of a royal family and that her cat was the pet they had treated as a deity. They lived a very isolated life together. Her presumed royal lineage was her excuse for not having many friends.

Without apparent reason, the woman constantly complained that she could never share what remained of this life with another cat, who would be just another stranger. This almost obsessive denial indicated that something was wrong here, and she probably had a strong subconscious doubt about her decision.

For a few months we worked on other personal matters unrelated to the death of her pet. Finally, it became apparent to her that she really wanted and needed another cat. In fact, she was desperate for one, but she could not admit it sooner.

We discussed the fact that the new cat would be a completely different personality, not a reincarnation of her previous pet. She seemed to accept this advice rather easily. Soon after this, using some mystical means of divination, she excitedly chose a kitten from a local animal shelter. Despite her formerly strong protests, getting another pet was, in this case, the best thing for this lonely woman. It should have been done sooner.

"All of God's Little Ones."   *Courtesy, Hartsdale Canine Cemetery, Inc.*

Memorial tree,
with individual
leaf inscriptions.
*Courtesy, Abbey Glen
Pet Memorial Park*

CHAPTER 12

Children
and the
Death of
a Pet

There is only one smartest dog in the world,
and every boy has it.

—Anonymous

*B*ereavement in children too often has been trivialized or given
inadequate attention and respect. We are so involved with
our own adult world of complexities and learned associations
that we tend to lose some perspective on how and why children
feel bereavement for a pet. Thus, we presume that it is advisable
to shelter them from this "grown-up" experience, which we find to be
very upsetting. In nearly all examples, that is absolutely the wrong
approach. If they are old enough to reason, then they sense very accu-
rately when they are being left out of important discussions about
things. In the death of a child's beloved pet, this matters a great deal.

HELPING THEM UNDERSTAND

It would be a great service to our children if we would step out of the restrictive mold of our traditional, non-thinking response to death. We have a strong obligation to them to begin their experience and knowledge of death in a constructive manner that is not as eva-sive and euphemistic as that which we grew up with. Each child, depending on the individual level of development, should be allowed to experience his or her own natural feelings of bereavement without being overprotected.

Children do not respond to death as adults do, unless they have been taught by example to behave this way. Their normal reactions are much more natural, curious and varied. There are several impor-tant factors affecting their diverse responses to bereavement. They are very intuitive, and are likely to sense when things about a pet's death are hidden. Sometimes this even becomes a sore spot for anger and resentment when they are older. Their age and maturity must be carefully considered when trying to work things out.

WHAT IS SAFE TO TELL CHILDREN?

Here we are very concerned with their ability to handle the major stress of facing death, especially the first time. Our overly protective tendencies may often prevent them from meeting this experience on their own terms. Because of our fearful preoccupations with death, we too easily overlook the simplicity of a child's levels of awareness and needs or responses to a pet's demise.

It is a natural instinct to protect children from facing stressful things in general and death in particular. Parents try carefully and, at times, excessively to ease or avoid their children's grief. Generally, young people are not permitted to attend funerals, wakes, burials or even memorial services. Nor are they allowed to visit anyone who may be dying. Children are shielded and not expected to be able to extend sympathy to others in bereavement. How then can they learn to have this for themselves, later in their lives, when their loved ones inevitably die? Because of unnatural protection and inter-ference, they have only minimal contact with death. They lack the firsthand experience that teaches a realistic understanding of death and bereavement.

Parents cannot really conceal their feelings from children. They are too intuitive and perceptive. But because of our attempts to exclude them from stressful events in our lives, they may respond in ways we do not expect. Feeling left out, they may secretly feel shame and guilt at not being worthy of our trust. They know when they are not included in what should be a natural family sharing of things, bad or good. Around age five this begins to matter. Of course, this age of readiness varies.

The general subject of death is not unknown to children. They watch movies and television, and they hear reports from their school-mates and friends. There is little that would really surprise them. In some ways, they are more sophisticated than we were at their age. It might astonish most parents how much children perceive. Depending on their age and experience, they are also somewhat aware of the taboo surrounding death and its discussion. Again, when they are excluded, they may feel guilty or that somehow it is their fault. Perhaps they have been "bad" again and don't remember how or why— as is so often the case with children.

Children are very pliant and can accept nearly anything if it is presented in simple, trusting ways. Any questions they may ask about a pet's death should be answered as honestly and simply as possible. Too often parents become very awkward or even embarrassed when it comes to discussing death, so they oversimplify, use trite euphe-misms or even lie to the child. "The dog is visiting someone, way out in the country, but it will be back later." "The dog is in the hospital, but it will be back soon." "The pet went on a trip." These are all examples of the evasions and lies that will slap back in everyone's face, sooner or later. Parents hope that the child will quickly forget and not challenge the idea. Children easily sense a betrayal of their confidence, which can permanently damage their image of a parent. That often is repressed and surfaces later in life as deep resentment and disappointment.

But the parents of a child will have even more trouble explaining death if they themselves have a problem with it. Children are very sensitive to this. Fortunately, they are resilient and accepting, and they perceive only as far as their limited understanding permits, at that time. Things that are complicated to us are frequently glossed over with no problem at all by them. They should never be lied to about things concerning the pet's death (but on very rare occasions, there can be valid exceptions to this). Try to explain to them what happened at a level that they can comprehend without distress.

For many possible reasons, children may not have adjusted to the prior death of a significant person in their lives. When this happens, there is no resolution. The child is actually in a state of arrested mourning. That is most likely the result of having been overprotected to a point where any later reference to death can be upsetting or frightening. Very often the household with a beloved pet presents an emotional time bomb to children with this problem. They will frequently create a fantasy world with the pet, constructing a personalized environment of love and security. If the pet should die before the child can resolve any earlier problems, a new level of stress will result. This may remain suppressed, or it may be suddenly expressed as secondary anger and grief, worsened by the first loss. Sudden behavioral problems always indicate there is something significant, that is deeply disturbing the child.

EXPLAINING A DEATH

How do you explain a pet's death to children? A good start is to find out what they think it means. Use that level of perception as your basis to start sketching out your answers. Don't try to explain fully. Most people cannot do so, anyway. You will be even more frustrated if you try, and children will sense this. That might also diminish their trust in your ability to help them.

Even if you work very hard at preparing a complicated or thorough explanation of the pet's death, it easily could be beyond the comprehension level of the child's developmental growth. Streamline your ideas, but not to the point of oversimplifying them or making them seem trivial to the child. Ask questions, and base what you say on what you learn from the level of the answers you get. Ideas that could be upsetting to adults are often glossed over by the youngster. To better understand how the child is responding, get some feedback at regular intervals. Ask him or her what is confusing or upsetting about the pet's death. Work on that at the child's level, not yours.

After a long and complicated explanation, the child may say something like this: "Oh, all I wanted to know is if my dog is in heaven." This demonstrates that explanations beyond a child's level and ability to understand may be lost on him or her. But don't misread this by being too simplistic. Such treatment may be deeply resented on a subconscious level of awareness. There are so many complicated reasons or explanations for things. But we must try to adjust our discussions about death to each individual's perceptions. Younger children are not so interested in adult detail or logic. They mostly seek easy, satisfying answers that address their current level of inquiry and awareness.

Try discussing pet death with your child. If it is at all possible, do this well in advance of the actual event. Most parents are surprised at the level of the child's awareness, openness and willingness to discuss this, even if it may be very simplistic. Such a discussion, of course, depends upon the child's emotional development and maturity. Even if the child doesn't seem to comprehend your strong feelings on the subject, this experience will provide a lesson in respecting emotions in others. You are a powerful role model to your child in everything you do or say.

In our culture, some bereavement problems result from the awkwardness or inability of individuals to respond to those in mourning. This happens because they generally don't know any better. An awareness of death probably had been withheld from them. Any experience or training in bereavement sensitivity may have been denied them as children. Now, as adults, they may become defensive, impatient or even critical of anyone bereaving for such a "trivial" matter as a pet.

How Do Children Accept Death?

Children do not accept death as adults do. They perceive concepts more at their surface values. They easily presume things, and tend to blame themselves for bad events that happen to the people and pets they love. It is not unusual for children to feel that they were naughty and that God or someone is punishing them for their behavior.

Children tend to suppress their guilt, fears and negative feelings because they do not know how to talk about them. Sometimes these escape from the subconscious and are expressed in upsetting dreams. Nightmares come from the repression of frightening ideas. They emerge with a vengeance during sleep, the time when restraints are gone. It is wise to avoid any possibly lurid or morbid details that concern the pet's death (or death in general). Alarming ideas may turn into misperceptions that could upset the child for the rest of his or her life.

Sometimes we are shocked by responses we never expected. It is important to never attempt to trivialize a child's grief as a means to ease it. Cases have been studied in which children believed that this reaction would also be their parents' response if they might die. That, of course, is the very opposite of what we want them to feel. Trivializing death reinforces and encourages insecurity. There are better ways to simplify and adapt ideas.

At a very young age, children should not be troubled with complicated explanations or discussions about euthanasia. But they should not be excluded or made to feel left out of family conferences, even at their young levels of comprehension. Let them sense how you respond to the death. They will use your example as a positive, safe role model and love you better for this.

Somehow, children must learn that death is the normal ending to life, just as birth is the beginning. Every living thing experiences both. It should be made clear that death can be very upsetting, but it is not bad, and it is not to be feared. Too often an irrational dread of death is unintentionally implanted, and this can disturb children for the rest of their lives. If you have strong religious views that help you ease your pain, then share these with the child. In issues dealing with death, children need and readily accept answers that are given with this feeling of authority.

Usually, a child has a very personal relationship with a pet. This is very different from what an adult experiences. In some cases, there can be almost a siblinglike attachment or understanding between them. Be frank with children, and stay at their levels of comprehension. Ask questions to get feedback and an understanding of how your attempt at communication is succeeding, or not. Share and guide, but don't shield children. If you make it easy for them to ask questions, they will be better able to grasp what they need to know. They also need to suffer some bereavement to be able to reach their own sense of closure.

THE SPECIAL ROLE OF A PET

Pets can be silly, childlike, playful and joyous. A pet makes a perfect companion for a child, who can learn trust and loyalty from the relationship. Pets provide a sense of security and continuity when the parents are not present. The animal friend is there for the child, no matter what the trouble or how badly he or she may have behaved—and the bond seems even stronger after a spanking or punishment.

Troubles are shared with these companion animals, who also serve as adoring siblings. In the long run, when a child cares for a pet, a healthy sense of responsibility and self-esteem develops. This becomes a basic component of the young person's self-image and attitude toward life. When that bond is finally broken by death, the child will respond in very personal ways that even a parent may not be aware of.

But what fun children have playing with their pets! There are very many pained adults undergoing psychotherapy who wish they could have had such a comfort and release. Children are not inhibited by the false sense of dignity that adults sometimes display. A pet supplies total security and love, and it does not judge or criticize. It gives a sense of complete acceptance and security, obeying and loving the child as nothing else can. It is loyal and will stay close and supportive during hard times. In all, the pet becomes a symbol of emotional security in an unsure world. Those are the wonder years for a child, before death changes everything.

WHAT CHILDREN MAY ASK

The kinds of questions most frequently asked by children include: "Where is my pet now?" "Why did she die?" "Is she happy now?" "Who takes care of her now?" "Will I ever see her again?" You must understand what the child is driving at and needs to know. Too often we answer in ways that do not satisfy the original question, as the child meant it.

Examples of bad and misleading answers to children include statements such as:

1. "Your pet was loved so much that God took it back to heaven." The child may wonder if God will take him or other dear members of the family back, as well.

2. "The animal doctor made a mistake and the pet died." A child may think that this may happen with people and their doctors, too.

3. "The pet ran away." This is tacitly understood by children to be untrue or improbable, at best. The child is being excluded from honest communication. Again, such an

attempt at deception may easily lead to distortions in the child's mind, causing feelings that he or she is undeserving or guilty and cannot be trusted with the truth.

4. "The pet got sick and died." The misperceived notion that dying is a result of getting sick may be very upsetting. Children and loved ones also get sick.

5. "The pet went to heaven" or "The pet went to sleep forever" can create frightening associations in a child's mind concerning heaven or even going to sleep.

Euphemisms such as, "The pet was put to sleep," have created frightening associations with sleep or surgical procedures during which a person has to be anesthetized. Attempts at sterilized verbal expressions can be all too quickly misunderstood by a child, who understands words more at their face value. At a young age, minds do not work as well in verbal metaphors.

Some of the upsetting and unexpected responses by children to the death of a pet have been, "I was bad, so my pet was taken," and, "If I am good, maybe he will come back to me." This is related to the bargaining phase adults may experience during early bereavement. What happened to the pet may convince the child that the world is not a safe place. Any such fears of insecurity will surely be triggered by future distressful experiences. They need to be addressed now. Family discord at this time will certainly hinder any adjustment to bereavement.

As we all know, a pet's disobedience sometimes causes its accidental death. There are countless examples of this. Obedience to authority is always part of any training, for a child or a pet. Certainly, no child is perfect in obeying rules. All youngsters experience some feelings of shame or guilt at this. It has been discovered that some youngsters secretly fear they may deservedly meet a similar fate—death—since they also disobey. Such a rationalized response instills an irrational fear, and it may remain with them for a very long time. There may even be times when it provokes disruptive social behavior, since the child feels he or she is already guilty and going to die anyway. Responsible parents should be sensitive to this and try to correct any misperceptions.

HELPING A CHILD ADJUST

One constantly hears of ideas and suggestions that have helped a child adjust to the death of a beloved pet. Some possible considerations include the following:

1. Hold a ceremony for the pet that includes the child and helps him or her bond more closely to the parents. This need not necessarily be at the gravesite. It serves to include the child in a positively structured bereavement activity. Shared rites and rituals on a very personal level help put the grief and death into some greater objectivity. Such an experience strengthens a child's sense of family and self-reliance during the mourning process. It also can aid in immunizing him or her from some of the scary, unspoken, subjective confusions of death that he or she will eventually run into.

2. Reminisce fondly with the child about the pet. Use pictures, if possible. Associate positive, happy events with the pet's memory. Emphasize that as long as we remember and love the pet, it will always be part of us. Associate happiness, not sadness with this.

3. Ask the local librarian to suggest children's books that include the death of a pet in the story line. There are growing numbers of these in print. Any competent book dealer can help, as well.

4. Discuss with the child the possibility of eventually getting another pet. Emphasize that this is not to try to replace the beloved pet or the memory, as that can never be done. This is to have another animal friend—but only when the child feels ready. Explain that it is like loving more than one person at a time. The new pet will be a different one, but the dead one is still loved and remembered. Suggest that when the new pet is very good, the child could tell it stories about the dead one and that they could have been wonderful friends if they had lived at the same time.

   Ask how the child feels about the pet's death and why. With older children, never argue about views you don't like. If there is a conflict between your ideas, suggest that you both think it over and discuss it again in a few days or so. *Be supportive but not critical.*

5. Visit an animal shelter with the child. Explain in advance that you will not adopt any animal during this visit. You are going for the special experience that only such a visit can give. Encourage the child to ask questions and make comments on what you both see. Discuss this experience later. This will help put the child's grief and needs into a much more objective perspective. It will ease the bereavement.

6. Inform the child's teacher about the death of the pet and its effect on the child. Ask for advice. You may get some good suggestions, based on sound developmental, educational training. But even if nothing new is suggested, you can feel more secure that the teacher will probably be paying special attention to the child's behavior and needs during this critical period. Ask that the teacher schedule a class discussion about pets and pet loss.

7. The child should have an opportunity to ask your family's veterinarian questions about the pet's death. You should be present to understand and add supportiveness and explanations, when needed.

8. In instances where euthanasia is necessary, include the child in a family discussion. Share and explain your thoughts and feelings. Keep the understanding at the child's level. Explain that different people react in many different ways to this loss. Each of us needs space, TLC and respect for our personal pain.

Of course, the death of a beloved pet presents problems even for a well-adjusted adult. But the child, who is inexperienced in this, looks to us for guidance in our words and deeds. Too often we are at a loss ourselves and may lose perspective on the effects of our behavior during this stressful time. Special care should be taken to be open, supportive and especially loving to children during what amounts to their bereavement, as well.

A comprehensive essay on children and the death of their pets would take a book to give the subject justice. This relatively short chapter is not an attempt to be all-inclusive. Considerations that may have been omitted are not necessarily of lesser importance. As in all studies of a psychological nature, there are so many possible varieties of experiences and responses.

The ultimate consideration here is that you are always the authority in your child's life, as well as the role model. See to it that the child feels included in your confidence. Treat the death of a pet with understanding, love and care, allowing the child to benefit from your example. The death of a pet should also be an instructive experience and may well help your young person endure the death of a significant human at some later date.

Children see tears and grief, and they learn firsthand what bereavement means. This can also sensitize them to the needs of others. Don't try to protect or shelter them from this reality. Let them share your feelings to a reasonable degree, according to their maturity and ability to understand. Share your experience and general responses with them, but always bear in mind that *you* are the example of how they are to behave. Avoid the mistakes that were made in your life, concerning the understanding of death. Children are the future, and we want them to be better and happier than we are.

"Enriching Our Lives."   *Courtesy, Hartsdale Canine Cemetery, Inc.*

CHAPTER 13

Euthanasia

*To every thing there is a season,
and a time to every purpose under the heaven:
a time to be born and a time to die.*

—Eccles. 3:1

*E*uthanasia is a matter of ethical and practical necessity. It is one of the most difficult decisions anyone can ever make for a pet who is a beloved friend. Although the decision is demanded by humanitarian obligation, it is always traumatic for the person who must finally make it. It is perhaps the ultimate heartbreak we must be willing to endure for our beloved companion animals.

Euthanasia provides necessary relief by ending terminal suffering and poor quality of life. This choice is highly subjective and often difficult to make. It is part of the ultimate responsibility of all pet keepers. We are morally obliged to protect and support the lives of our pets. Yet any compassionate necessity to end a pet's life must be addressed. Unfortunately, some pet stewards abuse this sacred trust.

Euthanasia is almost never a foreign concept to people. From our earliest days as pet keepers, most of us have given it some fleeting thought, unconsciously preparing for this possible need and eventuality. That, however, is only an abstraction before the grim reality. We are accomplished at not thinking about death, until we are forced by circumstances to face it.

A COMPLEX DECISION

Aside from being the right thing to do, euthanasia can be a psychological nightmare of confusion, guilt and final responsibility. To opt for it, you must truly believe that it is the only recourse to ease a pet's pain and suffering. Once you accept that, be steadfast in your belief that it is appropriate.

The fear of death can be immobilizing. Anticipation of the loss of the pet can be so overwhelming that one may delay making the necessary decision. But the pet suffers more than the owner. Fatal accidents and death while undergoing surgery sometimes take the responsibility of the decision away from us. Otherwise, we are honor-bound to exercise this ultimate trust and duty.

To some people, the decision to employ euthanasia is a convenience and is as easy and simple as throwing away an unwanted toy. To others it is a desperate, necessary resolution they want but cannot easily confront.

Fortunately, most of the rest of us fall somewhere between these two extremes. Choosing euthanasia is probably one of the most upsetting decisions one will ever have to make. But to own and care for a pet, one must accept the dreaded responsibility of possibly being forced to make this choice someday.

Aspects of Euthanasia

As difficult as it is, we must try to separate emotion from the decision-making process, when contemplating this necessary alternative. Keep in mind that there are three basic aspects of the awesome subject of euthanasia: practical, ethical and psychological. In most cases they are all vitally interrelated, and each can be overwhelming. From the practical point of view, euthanasia may be the only answer to how one should humanely terminate the degenerating quality of the pet's life.

It is practical to euthanize a dog who turns vicious. Here there is very little margin for an alternative choice. Another practical consideration can be that an owner may not be able to bear the overwhelming emotional stress caused by a slowly dying pet. The owner is in emotional agony, and he or she may dwell excessively on something that fosters a strong sense of guilt. The ethical aspects are theoretical and more easily accepted. They make perfectly good sense.

But the loving owner of a euthanized companion animal suffers deep psychological distress. Tragically, this beloved pet must have its life terminated by the one person who loves it most. This is both an irony of fate and an act of love, and the emotional strain is like nothing else.

In the long run, these considerations clearly demand that the question should no longer be concerned with *if* it should be done, but *when*. The psychology involved in making such a life-death decision is always disruptive, and sometimes the decision can be more easily made with the support of people who are close to you. Sometimes it is wise to get professional guidance or counseling if this decision proves to be very disturbing.

A Child's Perspective

As mentioned in the previous chapter, children should not be overprotected. They must not be made to feel left out of what may be very important to them. Their love of the pet should be respected by the parents. Depending on their age and ability to reason, they should be made part of what they feel is the decision-making process. Even if you have privately made up your own mind about what is to be done, make the children feel as though they have contributed good ideas to the discussion. Gentle persuasion is the rule here. Arguing with an older child about this sometimes causes emotional scars that last a lifetime.

MAKING THE DECISION

At what point has the quality of your pet's life degenerated to the critical point where you have the ethical responsibility and the obligation to end it? This is a terrible crisis for you, as well as your beloved pet.

Certainly, you should consult your veterinarian and others whom you trust to give objective, sound advice. One sometimes hears the suggestion to refer to an additional veterinarian for a second opinion. Although this has some merit, most practitioners will ask what the first one had said and will usually agree. Once the decision is made, the veterinarian and staff merely do the physical job. Most can give excellent advice on this, but there is often one around that does not.

As painful and difficult as it is, the final decision must be yours. The value of euthanasia is well accepted and appreciated, but the decision must never be arrived at hastily. Once acted on, it cannot be reversed. This is a terrible, heart-wrenching conclusion that has to be fully confirmed in advance. Once chosen, it must be embraced as the appropriate and final decision.

What should be the considerations for euthanasia during a medical emergency? If the pet is in terminal pain or bodily dysfunction, we owe that pet the dignity of a painless and dignified death. Since its end is imminent anyway, we can be more philosophical about it and accept it a little earlier. Is there any realistic chance of a spontaneous recovery or cure? How much pain is the animal in now, and will its suffering increase? Are the medical expenses absolutely prohibitive? What about the prolonged emotional strain on the owner, as well?

In considering euthanasia, we go through an intensely shocking decision-making period. During this time, the veterinarian may use some terms and euphemisms that the pet owner may not fully understand at this highly confusing and unstable moment. There have been cases in which clients have been told that their pet should be "put to sleep" or "put out of its misery." The pet was euthanized without the client's full understanding at the moment of what that meant. The intense guilt and anger that resulted from these instances could have been avoided. When we are very upset, we frequently do not comprehend metaphors well. We are more literal-minded and may entirely miss the point. This is another strong case against the use of euphemistic terminology and verbal manipulation.

Even when the word "euthanasia" is used, emotional blocks sometimes interfere with the full understanding of its meaning. In a denial of its necessity, we can set ourselves up for a terrible aftermath of guilt and soul-wrenching grief. We must be on top of the situation. It may be advisable to have someone you trust with you when you are faced with the decision. Later it is too late to change your mind. The suffering, terminally ill pet may be ready for it, but too often the owner is not.

The expression "putting an animal to sleep" is quite literal, in addition to being the most frequently used euphemism. This procedure is simple. The veterinarian painlessly injects a massive overdose of sedative or barbiturate intravenously. Some practitioners employ two different injections. The action of the first is to relax and sedate the pet;

the effect of the second is to stop the heart while the pet is asleep. Whatever suffering or discomfort it may have been experiencing up to that point is eased and released, as the animal quickly slips off into peaceful sleep and death.

As terrible and difficult as it is for each pet owner, most choose to be present for this simple, final procedure. They prefer to hold the pet in their arms, calming the animal and expressing their own final loving farewells and tears. The moment is so intensely personal and emotional that it often becomes overwhelming. It is an experience that is never forgotten.

Here, one's emotional composure is sacrificed as the last testimonial to their lives together. Intense personal grief is the price of this necessary, humane action. However, it is not uncommon to hear that this special moment together is sometimes experienced as a very spiritual, loving, transcendent episode. Many report that this unexpectedly gave them a profound and quieting sense of completion. So it may well not be so dreadful, after all.

If you opt for this act of mercy, it is good to close the book well. Say your personal, tearful good-byes. Understand that there is a unity in all things. When you die, your oneness with your beloved pet will be even more complete. But for now it must be over, except in your heart.

Yet, there are people who cannot bear to experience this, and there should be no shame in that. Witnessing the moment of death is far too upsetting for them. Unfortunately, it is not uncommon for many individuals who elect not to be present during that final moment to later regret the decision. This makes their bereavement worse because it adds the confusion of guilt and irrational reasons for grief. Opting to be present or not is a very painful and important decision that should take into consideration what is best for you, as well. But the pet's condition and needs must always have priority.

Most veterinarians find this procedure upsetting to perform, despite their frequent need to use it. A few, however, have developed an office rule that the pet owner may not be present during the actual procedure. Experience has taught them that people can suffer from a variety of unexpected, strong emotional responses.

Also, these veterinarians have a concern for financial liability. They may be sued. Some owners may faint, hurting themselves in the fall. Others might get hysterical, grow irrational or destructive or even suffer a heart attack from the unusual stress. It is best to discuss this first with your veterinarian and ask for advice. If it is necessary, you may have to choose another veterinarian for the procedure. But *you* should make the decision. You will have to live with the memory.

YOUR RESPONSIBILITY

In being the "provider of all things" to your pet, you have assumed a godlike role. From your pet's point of view, you are the source of everything and the cause of all that it understands. In addition to the love the pet knows, this includes everything from obedience, tricks and toys to food, medical care, shelter, company and *every* experience it has had.

But, as stated earlier, with this role you also took on the awesome responsibility of possibly having to make that final decision of life and death someday. As much as you don't want to have such an obligation, you do. There is no one else who has this moral and legal responsibility to decide or act accordingly. You must make that informed decision and be able to live with it later. And you have to be absolutely right in your conclusions, out of love for your pet as well as concern for yourself. Later on, this must not be distorted into some neurotic threat to your self-respect. The decision is always painful and fraught with emotional pitfalls. When done for the pet's benefit, it is always the right decision.

It is regrettable, but most organized religions use generalities and euphemisms regarding this relatively new problem of the death of pets. They find many reasons for sidestepping the issue and avoiding real answers. We are too often forced to make religious interpretations that fit the times but have no biblical precedent. Even if you are religious, what is wrong with "playing God" during an emergency if God doesn't act? Perhaps the deity sees it as your responsibility. There are many who now believe that the moral requirement demands humane action from the divinity within each of us. Chapter 16 offers innovative insights to this problem.

A PERSONAL DECISION

Before resorting to euthanasia, it is helpful, if time and circumstances allow, to consult as far in advance as possible with a few

116

trusted friends or family, as well as at least one veterinarian. Ultimately, however, this decision must be made subjectively in the deep-
est, most private, inner soul-searching you are capable of. The inti-
macy of your relationship with your pet may demand that no one else
can be part of this intense personal morality. But what should be fore-
most in your mind is the terrible negative change in the quality of life
of your pet.

Postponement may provide some more time for you, but is that the
proper concern? That can be really just another way of trying to avoid
and delay the inevitable. Such a stay is only temporary, at best, and
may only be serving a self-defeating denial of the grim reality. Thus,
the practical aspect usually helps make the decision for us. It then
becomes a matter of getting it done and evading the horror. If this
must be, then respect it. Honor your pet and yourself in this ultimate
private salute to the animal's life with you. Have it done right away.

When upset patients come to me after euthanizing their pets, they
always fall into one of two categories: those who agonize over having
possibly waited too long, or those who torture themselves for having
possibly done it too soon. But analysis has shown that all of these people had lifelong histories of indecision and self-doubt. As with other
unresolved problems, euthanasia served as a trigger mechanism to set
them off.

On the other hand, too many pet owners use euthanasia as an easy
way out of an uncomfortable stewardship. Unfortunately, they resort
to this procedure to terminate the life of an animal without serious
medical disorders—one who just does not behave the way they want
it to, or one who causes problems for them. Sometimes euthanasia is
decided on because people just don't want the pet any longer, and
euthanasia seems better to them than abandoning the animal or giving it to an animal shelter. There are qualified pet ethologists and
trainers who probably could remedy most problems, if consulted. But,
of course, there are all sorts of pet-owning people, as well as varied
responses to situations.

Because we cannot be spared from making this ultimate consideration, it is one of the most distressing actions we will ever have
to take. We should always bear in mind that no one else can legiti-
mately pass judgment on us for deciding on euthanasia. People should
respect our grief and painful decision with silence or supportiveness.
If there are some in our lives who are critical, we must be able to

ignore them, correct them or discard them. This is essential for our sake, as well as for the loving, living memory of our pet. However, beware of hasty emotional overreactions to these people.

ETHICAL CONSIDERATIONS

From the ethical point of view, do we have the right to take away life? In the animal and pet world, this was settled long ago, in the name of humane action. But it is argued that life is life, and the life of a beloved pet is in many ways equated with our own. Because there are still many who feel that we do not have the right to euthanize ourselves, this argument is weakly carried over to pets.

It is amazing to look at the history of American laws concerning cruelty to children. Essential new statutes were passed only on the strength of already existing laws protecting animals. These were the necessary legal precedents. We protected our animals better than we did our own young. Something is very wrong, here.

In the last few years, euthanasia has started to become a high profile issue for our self-treatment. Ironically, although "humane" action was originally intended for animals, not humans, there are still some who would not allow this on people, if they had the power. Keep your mind open. Whatever decision you make, if considering this necessary option for a pet, be sure it is your own, not someone else's. You will have to live with it after it is too late to change your mind. There always will be some who will criticize you, despite their lack of qualifications or right to do so. Let reality and compassion guide you in evaluating the situation and need for euthanasia. What is right cannot be called wrong, unless you are looking for justification to be miserable.

The concept of the living will is only a modern social phenomenon. The writer of such a document is, in effect, giving legal permission to be euthanized—given specific, dire medical circumstances. We have all read or heard of instances where people were kept on life-support machines for years, while actually being brain-dead or terminally comatose. The living will gives the individual some measure of protection in being able to decide how to die with dignity.

Shouldn't this respect also be exercised for our dear pets, as well? Who else but the loving pet owner has the moral right or responsibility to make such a judgment for them? The word "humane" takes on even stronger meaning in this context.

With the proper ethical safeguards and conditions, euthanasia is legal. It is also the most humane and moral ultimate decision we can make for ourselves and our beloved pets—who in many ways are extensions of ourselves. We are currently witnessing the curious social phenomenon of rapidly increasingly numbers of new cases of people who are writing living wills for themselves. But many do this only after first experiencing the soul-wrenching ordeal of having to euthanize a beloved pet. The analogy seems clear here. Our beloved companion animals teach us many things, and this is one of the most amazing.

In the final analysis, if the decision to euthanize a pet is made for the right reasons, there can be no legitimate challenge to its morality and ultimate ethical nature—even from the narrowest of religious or even bigoted interpretations. Is it not vile and immoral to condone and perpetuate pain and suffering? Is the decision to euthanize a pet less necessary or moral than that for a human? Can we ethically sidestep this responsibility? The time for moral cowardice is over. We must make the right decision now.

Sometimes we experience a delayed reaction. Perhaps the least considered and the most striking effect of having euthanized a pet is the sudden onset of unexpected depression and feelings of guilt. Being human, we suffer and are bereft at the death of a loved one. But we can also create unnecessary torment in our lives, and that is always a mistake.

There are instances of people later regretting having agreed to euthanasia while they were under great stress. This should be an informed decision, made beforehand—or after a reasonable waiting period, if possible. In some instances, however, the correctness of the decision is not really the issue. Selfish preoccupation with their own feelings is the most important consideration for these individuals. The pet comes only after themselves, in every circumstance. Other bereaved pet owners may be ambivalent and insecure, lacking emotional stability because of the pressures at the moment. Often there are additional underlying reasons for this, with secondary guilt present.

A HUMAN RESPONSE

We all respond individually, and sometimes irrationally. The death of a loved one will put us into a state of mourning. Whether the end

This memorial statue, by French sculptor Jules Moignez, entitled "Pointer Marking a Pheasant," was valued at $25 when purchased by Geraldine Rockefeller Dodge in 1921. Valued at over $4,000 in 1976, it now graces the entrance to St. Hubert's Giralda, an animal shelter, museum and education center on the grounds of the former Dodge estate in New Jersey.

Courtesy, St. Hubert's Giralda

was spontaneous or humanely produced, the human equation is not changed. Because of the intensity of our emotions, the clarity of our thinking is usually lost for a brief while. The confusions of guilt often distort our lives. Guilt is one response to handling responsibility and not being able to bear up under it.

The subject of death has always upset, intimidated and confused us. Who is to say what it really is or what it means? In our frightened search for insight into the unknown, assurance and justification often elude us. Being forced by love and morality to become the angel of death for our pets is often overwhelming, or unsettling at best. But it serves two necessary and good purposes: We do what is right for the pet, and we ourselves are forced into an enormous existential growth step. We go on.

Those who suffer most terribly in this role frequently created their own pitfalls by having allowed themselves to become too emotionally dependent on their pets. Sometimes our intense love for our companion animals eclipses much of the responsibility and love we should have for ourselves. Intimate lifestyles and complex psychological interdependencies affect each of us in different ways and degrees.

The beloved pet frequently becomes an means of unconscious escape from a deep personal need or inadequacy. We allow our animal friends to give us a sense of personal transcendence. This is not at all unusual, but it is seldom recognized and rarely admitted. In many ways, the relationship may be more intimate than with other humans.

All humans experience some neurotic needs, each one very personal and unique. These responses can span the spectrum from harmless to pathological. The real measure of our "normalcy" is how we respond to stimuli, while maintaining our usual lifestyle. Since pets become extensions of ourselves, their innocence in such a world of complexities and troubles often represents the good part of ourselves, which we inwardly love and isolate. This constant supportiveness from a pet may offer a small escape from disagreeable reality. The interrelationship between master and pet often becomes a living exercise in creative fantasy, as well as improved self-esteem. Thus, the decision to euthanize can be all the more agonizing.

There is another important consideration in the decision process that must be addressed here. There are some unique situations where the pet's degenerated quality of life may not yet be fatal. But the extreme heroic measures that are required to maintain this strained life could prove to be too oppressive to the pet owner, emotionally or financially. That also becomes a valid and legitimate consideration in whether to euthanize. At what time may pet owners stop sacrificing their *own* quality of life to temporarily hold off the inevitable? Again, only the individual may make a legitimate judgment on this. It can be a heartbreaking compromise.

By having to become the angel of death to that beloved pet and extension of ourselves, we are each tasting a bit of our own death. And that is always very upsetting. We are forced back to the reality of being truly alone on our life journey, despite all the friends and family we may have.

In having to euthanize, we must come to an existential turning point in our lives, ever seeking self-understanding and justification. In meeting ourselves in this darkness, we learn that we can go on. We are strengthened by that particular living, loving enrichment that we shared for a few wonderful years with our beloved pet. Now we have to be better because of that wonderful experience.

WHAT DO ANIMALS EXPERIENCE?

Some people fear that their pets know what is going to happen when they take them out on that final trip. The companion animals may sense that their time has come and that their human companion is helping them. There have been reported cases in which a pet who was about to be euthanized showed signs of being greatly upset because the owner was in another room. In all cases, when that person joined the pet and veterinarian, the animal grew calm and waited to be helped out of all its pain and misery. It seems that they need us for this parting.

The pet may seem anxious, but that is almost always because it recognizes the veterinarian's office and smells the fear of other animals. It will also be sensitive to the owner's intense feelings at this time, and it may react nervously in response to them. But it is not fearful of dying. So far as we know, with the exception of only some of the higher primates, animals are not upset at the prospect of their own death. When their time comes, they sense it and often go off by themselves, accepting death as normal. They do not get morbid or sentimental about it. Only humans do that. We find their acceptance of death dif-ficult to accept, and we embellish or distort the reality to make ourselves feel better. We are often guilty of ascribing human feelings or emotions to our pets. That is always a mistake, but most people do it.

Our pets do not get upset at the prospect of their own death. That is a figment of our imagination and has become one of the more unnerving misperceptions that people have. When we assign our fear of death to our pets, we are romantically and inaccurately attributing human qualities to them. In reality, at this time there is no regret or sadness in their minds. Those feelings are ours, exclusively, in our relationship with the pet. We should not torture ourselves during our grief by agonizing about this and distorting our final memories of our beloved companion animals.

ADDITIONAL THOUGHTS

With all of our humanitarian considerations, there are still some who claim that euthanasia is always wrong. These people are usually the "holier than thou" type and feel that they are superior to others in their moral, religious and ethical values. That is nonsense.

While considering euthanasia and its critics, we also have to be concerned with the killing of other animals. What about proposed slaughterhouse reform? Don't we have a moral obligation to act to remedy these daily horrors? Or is it easier to turn our backs on this? As stewards of all other life on this planet, don't we have a responsibility to prevent the cruel conditions and very inhumane ways of "dispatching" these other animals?

Have you become aware of the rapidly increasing trend toward vegetarianism? Why are so many people turning away from eating animals?

Did you ever think that even the bait worm is screaming on the hook, but you can't hear it—and won't allow yourself to observe or even acknowledge its agony?

If an individual is not concerned with these and similar considerations, then the argument can be made that *that* person has no moral right to criticize or oppose euthanasia.

Much of the world remained passive to the Nazi holocaust while it was rampant. And many of the same horrors are being committed to-day in several parts of the world. If any individual can turn away from these with "studied ignorance," preferring to remain noncommittal, then what happens to that person's claim to be able to ethically judge or condemn euthanasia?

Humane care is for humans, as well as for pets and other animals. Perhaps we are in some danger of losing this vision. It is never too late to become involved or to become an evolved human. The movement grows. Each of us grows. The life and death of all animals is our moral concern and responsibility. Even the Bible says that man is the steward of all the animals.

In this grievous forced encounter with death, we can learn new things. But there are answers to some personal problems about pet death, bereavement and euthanasia that cannot be satisfied by this or any other book. We must reach down deep into our innermost selves for the real answers.

CHAPTER 14

Final

Arrangements

Break, break, break at the feet of they crags, O sea! But the tender grace of a day that is dead will never come back to me.

—Alfred, Lord Tennyson

We love our pets dearly, and we go well out of our way to see that they get everything they could possibly need or want. It can be said that America is a nation of pets, and we treasure them above even jewels. Astonishing published figures show that people all over the world spend about $10.8 billion annually on the purchases of gem diamonds. Yet in 1997, Americans spent over $20 billion on food and veterinary care just for cats and dogs. And that number is constantly growing with the increasing numbers and varieties of animals in our pet population.

The annual dollar amount spent in the United States on mortuary care for all pets has been roughly estimated at between $6 to $9 million, but pet cemeteries have existed here for over a century. In the last twenty years or so, their numbers have rapidly increased, and there are now three major associations to promote their quality and service. Judging by the careful maintenance and respect for the innumerable gravesites in these establishments, it is obvious that the loving care we give our pets does not end when their lives do. Their

A devoted pet ever mourned.   *Courtesy, Hartsdale Canine Cemetery, Inc.*

Ossuary for beloved cremains.   *Courtesy, Abbey Glen Pet Memorial Park*

cherished memory lives on in us, and it seems fitting that we memo-rialize their remains the same as we do our dearly departed fellow humans.

We learn from our mistakes, though, and have come to realize that looking for a cemetery or crematorium just after the pet's death can be the hardest and most inefficient way to go about this task. And it could also prove to be the most expensive. Generally, it makes more sense to get an overview of the establishments that are available in your immediate area and the services they provide. Long before you pet's death is the best time to obtain option and price brochures. Charges may vary from place to place. If you don't know how to find these establishments, check out the Yellow Pages in your local tele-phone directory; look under "Pet Cemeteries and Crematories." Information is also available free, on request, by contacting the listed associations of pet cemeteries, found in the appendix. Your veteri-narian should also be able to give you some suggestions, without hav-ing to make a profit on this. Ask him or her. Keep in mind, though, that most veterinarians receive a referral fee from the cemetery or crematory that they send the bodies to. So your best interest may not be served in this manner. Also check out your local SPCA or Bide-A-Wee Foundation, if there is one in your vicinity. Fellow pet own-ers are another good source of information regarding pet burial or cremation.

All of this advanced preparation may seem a bit unsettling to the owner of a new pet, who probably hates giving even a brief thought to its eventual death. This makes perfectly good sense. However, checking these things out beforehand can sometimes be an amazing stimulus to loving one's pet even better than before. Whatever your action or inaction on this early preparation, it is important to know in advance not to be caught totally unprepared and ignorant when that time actually comes—and it will. This chapter will also help you with your selection, if it isn't already too late.

BURIAL OPTIONS

Several options are available in the handling of the deceased pet. As with humans, burial and cremation are two choices. Now with pets there are new choices—freeze-drying and taxidermy. These choices may seem repulsive to many, but there are always some who will opt for them.

There have been recent developments in the freeze-drying of animal corpses, which seems to preserve them perfectly. Sometimes this is combined with taxidermy for added durability and realism. The rationale behind this is that some people would love to have their pet still with them, in body if not in spirit. This can seem a bit ghoulish to many, but who is to criticize anything benign if it makes people feel better? These services are advertised in pet mortuary publications and can be located through most of them. These services may even be listed in your local Yellow Pages by now.

Burial is the most common preference, but it can get complicated. Most people like to bury their pets in very private sites on their own property. That makes excellent sense, but unfortunately it is illegal in most of the country. But this is "more honored in the breech than in the observance." Laws are supposed to be made to serve us, not the reverse. Nevertheless, check out your local statutes on this. It is remotely possible that variations exist in your favor.

Today there are many pet cemeteries throughout the world. Most of them seem to be in the United States, however. As a rule, these cemeteries are spacious, beautifully landscaped and legitimate. Most of them also take pains to have legal provisions against the land ever being reused in the future for any other purpose. Whenever visiting or inquiring, ask what guarantees they provide, if any, regarding this very important matter. Occasionally we read in the papers about a pet cemetery that is being dug up to make way for "development." We don't want that for our pets! If the cemetery cannot provide written documentation of legal protection from this, walk away. But destruction of pet cemeteries is becoming more of a rarity today, among the more professional ones. Be wary, though.

If a burial is chosen over the other options, then you have additional considerations and expenses to deal with. Prices range widely, for coffin and gravestones, according to size, materials and workmanship. Just as with human burials, you must make personal decisions depending on what you want, and can afford. But if you had time to comparison shop earlier, a good bit of money may be saved. Some places are just more expensive than others. But as mentioned earlier, immediately after the pet's death is not the right time to have to make these kinds of difficult decisions—just as with human burials. The legitimate pet cemetery will not pressure you to make an immediate choice.

You will probably want to hold some sort of private service at the gravesite. Some places charge for this, while others don't. Sometimes it is good to have this led by a professional, especially when the mourner is so distraught as to be a bit dysfunctional for that moment. But the most touching memorial services I ever attended were conducted privately, with plenty of tears and hesitations.

If you can organize a funeral in advance, invite a very limited group to attend. Make sure that this includes only people who hold the same views as you do regarding the loss of a beloved pet. It can be very upsetting to have someone present who may feel you are being overindulgent with such a ceremony. Such people stand out badly, and the ceremony is diminished because of them. Definitely bring the children who loved the pet. If you can, say some prepared thoughts about the pet and your special love for it. Tell everyone *why* you loved it so very much. It will make you cry and lose control for the moment, but it is good. If you need to, read your thoughts from a paper you have prepared in advance. Nobody will mind. Sometimes religious considerations will be brought into the service. That is a personal decision. Regardless of its design or handling, you will feel much better having the memory of such a service.

More and more people today are opting for cremation of their own bodies after death. This is becoming increasingly popular for pets, as well. At the present time, about 45 percent of pet deaths are treated in this manner. It has some advantages that you may wish to consider. Starting at the very beginning, cremation is another service your veterinarian can help provide. Of course, there will be a kickback fee. Pet funeral parlors, cemeteries and crematoriums will also offer these services at varying prices. They will most often be lower than if you had signed a contract with the veterinarian.

Most humane societies, as well as pet cemeteries and some veterinary clinics, operate their own crematoriums. They usually provide informative brochures that you should obtain well in advance of any need for their use. The choice of individual or communal cremation is explained.

The ashes may be buried in the same way that a body is buried. Some cemeteries reserve special sections just for this type of interment. Others will allow either type of burial anywhere on the premises. It was interesting to learn that in most states people may have their own ashes buried along with those of their pet or pets. The law is not so restrictive in the burial or disposal of cremains. The interment of bodies is another matter.

There are two basic types of cremation services available. The mass cremation is the less expensive, of course. This is when your pet's body is incinerated with many other pets, and its ashes are returned to you. The other option is the more costly private procedure. Many people prefer this for a few reasons. It is not shared with others, and you are less prone to worry that the ashes (cremains) are not wrongly identified or mixed up with another pet's.

You will also need to choose the kind of container to keep the ashes in. Keep in mind that this is a business, so the styles, sizes and prices will vary. There is nothing wrong with keeping the cremains in a cardboard box for burial or scattering. It certainly is not disrespectful to your pet. This is purely a personal decision, and nobody will judge you by your choices.

Most pet cemeteries have columbariums (ossuaries) where the cremains are stored permanently in prominent vaults. Of course, that is an additional expense, but it might be just the thing you feel comfortable with. Some of these are quite beautiful and worthy of their precious contents.

Private cemetery costs vary from a few hundred dollars and up. Options of community or individual burial are offered by many pet cemeteries and humane societies (such as the Bide-A-Wee Foundation). These nonprofit humane societies provide similar memorial facilities that are considerably less expensive, while preserving the dignity of your pet's memory. Your veterinarian should be able to advise you about this, but always keep in mind that there is a profit incentive here. It is always wise to contact other pet owners for advice.

If you should have a reasonably strong feeling about what action or selection to take, don't hesitate. Put it into effect right away. You may get well-intended conflicting and disturbing opinions later. What other people may think should be of lesser value than your own feelings and well-considered decision.

At present, there is only one pet cemetery in the United States that has adjacent plots for pets as well as their owners. This cemetery is called the Bonheur Memorial Park, in Elkridge, Maryland. Most states and communities outlaw this practice. Indeed, as stated earlier, in most areas of the country, people may not even legally bury a beloved pet on their private property.

INVESTIGATE WITH CARE

Caveat emptor! "Let the buyer beware." You should know that some pet cemeteries and mortuary facilities have been run by unscrupulous, unfeeling people. This is increasingly rare, today, but all it takes is one! These few scoundrels deliberately mislead and cheat the credulous pet owner, who unfortunately is not in any position to objectively evaluate things at the time of bereavement. This corruption of an otherwise honorable profession has been prosecuted in court and found guilty of violating many laws. They are con artists—deliberate criminals who prey on very susceptible people at their most vulnerable time. But they get rich quickly as a result of their vile scams.

In 1991, there was a scandal involving a pet cemetery in Long Island, New York. Heartbroken mourners who believed their pets had been buried or cremated according to contract were shocked to discover that there were really mass burial pits. These contained the unprotected decomposing bodies of beloved pets who were supposed to have been treated in completely different ways. These cemetery profiteers were tried and found guilty on several counts of criminal behavior. They were also sued in civil courts by thousands of bereft pet owners. Although these criminals served jail terms, the irreversible damage had been done. Admittedly, this is a rare example, but it may not be the last one. To their credit, most pet cemeterians now try to police their own industry in order to prevent this sort of thing from ever happening again.

It would be completely wrong to brand the entire pet mortuary profession with the same stamp. Most of these businesses are very moral with fine reputations. Some have been in existence nearly a century. They are eager to prove their legitimacy. Most families have human burial plots already assigned to their still living members. Why wouldn't this make sense for pets, as well?

VISITS

It is good to visit any pet cemeteries that are in your vicinity. Walk around. Look and feel how other loving pet owners have felt. Read the inscriptions. You will be moved and strengthened by them.

If possible, it is a very moving occasion to visit an older, well-established pet cemetery. The aging and varied grave markers, stones and monuments, along with their heartfelt inscriptions, are a powerful testament to our love of all types of pets. Many family burial plots have impressive markers and inscriptions memorializing different pets who belonged to the same owner or family over time. Each of these was buried years apart, and the stone was inscribed accordingly. In these serene places, there is a sense of community and intense loving experiences that are shared joyously. This will be an experience of great positive value to you, regardless of how you decide to care for the body of your beloved pet. There are no other places like these.

In 1986, a team of archaeologists unearthed a pet cemetery in Ashkelon, a port city of the Persian Empire that had been inhabited by people in what is now southern Israel. The skeletal remains of about one thousand dogs, from puppies to old ones, were found. They had been individually buried over a long period of time. The cemetery dated back to what is called the Persian Period, which lasted from about 500 to 332 B.C. All indications suggest that each dog freely roamed a sacred precinct and died of natural causes. The plots had been cared for and protected from scavengers and human interference. This unexpected find is the oldest surviving record of a pet cemetery ever discovered. But these dogs were not actually pets.

From ancient Egypt there are even older remains of individually mummified dogs and cats, along with their carved and inscribed sarcophagi and wooden coffins.

MAKING A FINAL DECISION

If you have just experienced the death of a beloved pet and are faced with the need to make an immediate decision, delay it at least for a few hours. Talk with trusted, concerned people. Ask them about their feelings and opinions. In addition to these people whom you know, there are professionals at the pet cemeteries and pet funeral parlors who are usually well-prepared to give you sound advice and counseling. Although they also want to sell you a product, for the most part they are very good at what they do. If you have certain financial or other limitations, explain this to them. These people are pet lovers and humanitarians. They really want to help. Don't hesitate to say when you are not comfortable with anything they suggest. A good pet cemetery or funeral parlor has a reputation to make and keep, which can be to your advantage at this time. But to feel safe, be sure your final decision is your own, regardless of who does or doesn't agree with it.

In the long run, all of this is only a temporary turbulence in your life. Whatever final arrangements you decide on, they will be made with your undying love. And that is the greatest memorial anyone can ever give.

Here is text taken from a memorial:

" . . . *For if the dog be well remembered, if sometimes she leaps through your dreams actual as in life, eyes kindling, laughing, begging, it matters not where that dog sleeps. On a hill where the wind is unrebuked and the trees are roaring, or beside a stream she knew in puppyhood, or somewhere in the flatness of a pastureland where most exhilarating cattle graze. It is one to a dog, and all one to you, and nothing is gained and nothing lost—if memory lives. But there is one best place to bury a dog.*

"If you bury her in this spot, she will come to you when you call—come to you over the grim, dim frontiers of death, and down the well-remembered path and to your side again. And though you may call a dozen living dogs to heel, they shall not growl at her nor resent her coming, for she belongs there.

"People may scoff at you, who see no lightest blade of grass bent by her footfall, who hear no whimper, people who have never really had a dog. Smile at them, for you shall know something that is hidden from them.

"The one best place to bury a good dog is in the heart of her master."

Anonymous

"A Gift of Love Memorial"—testimony to many pets who enriched their owners' lives.

Courtesy, Abbey Glen Pet Memorial Park

Memorial to fire dogs.   *Courtesy, Bide-A-Wee, photo by George Wirt*

CHAPTER 15

Supportive
Counseling

Sweet are the uses of adversity.

—*William Shakespeare*

The loss of a pet is an extremely difficult subject that traditionally has been glossed over for many reasons. Aside from
the intolerant criticisms of the arrogant few who claim that
this loss means nothing, we live in a society that passionately avoids
thinking or speaking about "any" death. Even the word and concept
have been avoided and replaced with polite, more socially acceptable
expressions. In many circles we must not even use the words "die" or
"death," and we are required to avoid many other direct terms, as
well. It becomes necessary to say something such as "pass away" or
"gone on to his/her maker." As mentioned in previous chapters, we
still tend to hide behind euphemisms and avoidance. Despite our feelings of condolence when someone else grieves over any death, we
tend to remain cautiously apart. Death scares us, and we don't know
how to handle it.

Psychologically, we feel threatened and unable to cope with this
subject that nobody wants to talk about. It is a topic that most
people are terribly uncomfortable with. People don't know how to
examine their feelings about death without confusion, embarrassment

and even fear. Our culture has evolved many taboos concerning our responses. Euphemisms ease our somewhat Victorian reluctance to deal with these upsetting and unacceptable words or ideas. This foolish consistency is a self-made hobgoblin still mocking us, even now at the end of the twentieth century.

TRADITIONAL RESPONSES

Death is too upsetting a subject, and Western society has traditionally avoided it as much as possible. We leave its handling to the professionals—the clergy and mortuary specialists. Since nobody knows the answers or even the right questions, we tend to evade its consideration or discussion, keeping our private passions, hopes and heartbreaks to ourselves. When it comes to the death of a beloved pet, however, there is the additional problem of being intimidated by those who tend to belittle any grief that we may feel for the loss of a "mere animal." Up until recently, it was tacitly accepted by nearly everyone, including the bereaved, that there must be something wrong with us if we behave so "badly" for a pet. But the reality is that the death of any loved companion, pet or person, will cause bereavement and personal grief. People with little or no compassion take a perverse pleasure in criticizing others for their feelings. Almost invariably, these self-styled critics lack sensitivity or do not understand this experience, and they are too quick to condemn others. Yet, in our grief, we still try to hide our feelings from people who have prejudices. We owe these critics nothing, but of course we are vulnerable, especially during this period of intense heartache. It is natural to want to hide this insecurity.

Since our Western concept of death is upsetting to so many, it was generally presumed that the death of only a pet should, naturally, be less meaningful than that of a human. Grief for a pet was an easy emotion to criticize. Bereaving pet owners in the midst of their overwhelming grief had to become defensive and apologetic, for fear of being ridiculed and ostracized. But now, at last, because of broadened exposure to these experiences, the mass media are starting to cover the subject of pet death with an increasing sense of humanism and awareness. When so many people experience this kind of grief each year, it becomes a major social phenomenon that gradually must make itself better understood, despite all the traditional pitfalls.

You are not alone in your grief. The time has finally come to realize and accept this. There are millions of us, and our numbers are ever increasing. Because of the escalating visibility of such experiences, the problem is becoming much more accepted as a normal living experience. Bereavement for a beloved pet is no longer ridiculed and ignored, as it had been. Indeed, in some small circles it is even becoming an honored and respected experience. Unfortunately, this is a rite of passage for pet lovers everywhere. In our roles as loving stewards we must learn the pain of having to let go when the time comes. The rewards far outweigh the costs.

THE FIRST BEREAVEMENT CLINICS

The first four pet bereavement clinics in the country were established in the 1980s, and they were an immediate success. Only ten years later, about twenty five major pet bereavement clinics, with specially chosen counselors, have been established around the United States (with more being planned). Now nearly every large city in the country has some social worker or trained psychotherapist offering help in this newly recognized category. Good old pragmatic Yankee ingenuity is one of our national hallmarks. Necessity has always been the mother of invention here.

CHOOSE WITH CARE

Now there are hundreds of other people suddenly appearing on the pet bereavement scene. Although most of them are very well-intentioned, they have little or no appropriate training or experience and are calling themselves pet bereavement counselors. They love animals, have good hearts and are driven by differing very personal motivations to help other people control their lives.

Unfortunately, among these many, there are some who have extremely unusual views and feelings about life. Their varied passions for such esoteric interests as crystals, aromas, pyramids, aliens, numerology, astrology, seances and so on have convinced them that they can help soothe the aching heart of the person bereaving for a pet. There is an amazing spectrum of arcane approaches, some of which may be effective while others may well cross the border into some form of self-delusion or even harmless psychosis. Although they themselves are in no apparent danger from this, the people they counsel may be placed in jeopardy.

It must be admitted that an approach to counseling in pet bereavement based on radical religious or "spiritual" views may well work wonders for a small population of mourners. But the approaches that rely, for example, on candles and chants under a pyramidal structure raise many doubts. Of course, a "placebo effect" can work wonders under the right conditions. If the client truly believes a treatment will work, the healing may actually occur.

There is an astonishing variety of approaches being offered by this influx of well-intentioned people. It is also unfortunate that these people use no discretion when selecting their clients. Too many of these consultants will try to prescribe their mystical approaches to anyone who is grieving for a beloved pet, regardless of that person's beliefs or attitudes. Under conditions of such stress and grief, these consultants take unfair advantage of their clients' extreme vulnerability by imposing such strong personal views on them. This can be seen as an ego trip and expression of power in an extremely sensitive emotional environment. It also violates basic counseling standards and ethics, and in some cases, it can do great harm. On a few occasions I have been called in on emergency sessions to do damage control. As indicated in previous chapters, people under severe stress may have repressed acute psychological problems that are triggered by just this kind of emotional intensity. Clients who are prone to hysterics, suicide or aggravated depression are especially endangered by these self-styled counselors who do not know the danger signs. Actually, some of these consultants are in actual denial about the limits of their ability to help or damage. A well-intentioned self-image as a healer is not enough in this case.

In most states, no regulations exist to prevent anyone from hanging up a shingle as a "psychotherapist." That is bad enough, but now along come all these hundreds of others who are starting to call themselves "pet bereavement counselors." Unfortunately, there are no standards or requirements of any kind, and anybody can do this! One need not even have a grammar school education for this. The final choice in counselors should always be up to the enlightened prospective client, though.

But to be fair, even licensed psychiatrists with M.D. degrees may not be good for this still new and very specialized field. There have been cases when patients of such reputable practitioners have found it necessary to find experienced pet bereavement counselors who knew how to help them. Book training and degrees do not create a compatible or sensitive personality. Other personal qualities based on loving animals and people are absolutely essential. Sometimes, even these much more radical practitioners have a better grasp of the problem and can relate more naturally with their clients. Some important human qualities cannot be created by university diplomas. We have a very strange mixture of mentors, indeed.

A good counselor must be a pet lover, just for starters. He or she must also have reasonable training and experience in the loss of a pet. And then there are the other less definable personal characteristics that make up what we call charisma, or a "bedside manner." Then there has to be a reasonable level of respect and chemistry between counselor and client. Some people are natural advisors, and others will never be, despite degrees, education or even experience.

The honor of being called a healer is a great one, indeed. It is one of the finest compliments anyone can be given. This is an achievement that takes a long time to accomplish. In addition to loving what one does, the practitioner must be absolutely certain that the method really does work. There is no room for doubt or self-deception. Dedication to the cure, not the method, is the earmark here. Unfortunately, too many who counsel in pet bereavement do not measure up to this requirement—regardless of their credentials, or lack of them. But there are many good, concerned, "everyday" people who successfully help others. It is heartening and inspiring to realize that the ranks of these humanists are increasing.

A Growing Support

Starting in the early 1980s, we have seen a growing and open support for pet bereavement. This all too human expression used to be socially frowned upon. What we really have here is the beginning of a revolution in thinking and public attitude. Others are beginning to realize that mourning is not a privileged commemoration reserved only for the loss of human loved ones.

History, art and literature provide us with many glimpses into personal memorials to beloved dogs. These emotional expressions generally have been accepted because of their great human-interest value. The concept of a hero weeping for a faithful dog is dramatic and even poetic. It has a classic and universal appeal to our basic love of all animals.

As household pets became more common, the problem of bereavement for them increased greatly. This once occasional, secret tragedy has become something very different with time. Now we are faced with the misfortunes of great masses who must deal with this shock. The rarity has gradually evolved, as pet bereavement started being perceived as a common experience. Despite this, many individuals still tend to hide their distress from those who have no understanding or sensitivity to their problem. As with some other important contemporary social issues, pet bereavement is finally "coming out of the closet."

SEEKING HELP

Most often our grief responses need sharing and good counsel. That certainly does not mean that one is in need of professional guidance. However, if we do opt for trained help, it does not imply that we are weak or emotionally defective. On the contrary, when we seek answers and objectivity, it may be a sign of good mental health. Professional guidance could offer just the boost we need in helping ourselves attain some positive direction during this particular time of trial and suffering.

We need tender loving care and good people around us during this personal crisis. Anyone who is truly sympathetic can be a good listener. We need people around us now, but it is necessary to avoid the company of those who cause stress.

There are some helpful practices the person in mourning should consider:

1. If you live alone, try to change your daily patterns slightly. Try to be with others more often, and stay away from sad and unhappy people.

2. Watch different television programs, and listen to other radio stations.

3. Avoid certain types of movies that may be upsetting, and actively seek out others that are entertaining. Enjoy them with someone who is supportive of what you are going through.

4. Although you may feel some initial resistance, arrange to visit or go out more frequently or even on a regular basis.

You can still take memories with you and share them, if you choose.

5. At this time, avoid any situations that may prove upsetting.

6. Meet with other pet owners and talk about what you are going through.

7. Attend pet bereavement support group sessions. They are a wonderful sharing and healing experience.

COUNSELING

Earlier, professionals with psychological and psychiatric training had not been forced to consider the complexities of pet bereavement. The truly understanding counselor used to be a rare, personal treasure. Unfortunately, many of these professionals with no personal experience or understanding of pet bereavement offer their general well-intended guidance that is often too shallow and inadequate. Not being pet-people themselves, they lack a basic understanding of the love that others have for their pets. Now this is starting to change for the better. At the time of this writing, there is only one facility organized to train professional counselors in pet bereavement. The Association for Pet Loss and Bereavement was recently formed in order to serve this and other related needs. This association is listed at the end of this chapter.

Today, the specialty of health and death care for pets has become a multi-billion-dollar business. With such increased visibility and growing socio-economic pressure, it is natural that there should now be a much greater positive response to the needs of so many. Unfortunately, in the past, this had always been rare. Even veterinary colleges used to give little instruction, or none at all, on death counseling and sensitivity. Now that is all changing. Within the past decade or so, there has been a growing movement to correct this condition to better provide for the bereaving pet owner. Veterinary colleges and pet hospitals have recognized this perception and the need to train themselves, as well as the general public.

It used to be that the only source of advice was pet mortuaries, where the sheer volume of varied experiences with bereaved pet owners had created a collective base of wisdom and philosophy. These establishments may help with good, practical advice and support, but their business is the mechanics of burial or cremation. Indeed, some clients still hesitate to ask for help there because they feel that the interest of these places is strictly that of a financially motivated business. In some instances this is true, but there are many wonderful exceptions. Aside from all the other counselors, professional pet cemeterians have a great deal of experience and compassion, and they can be very supportive. Some of them have even received training in counseling. This is something you can ask about when you visit or call.

THE HUMANISTIC VIEW

The growing humanistic view of bereavement places mourners and their pain as the prime focus, with all other considerations secondary. There is absolutely no tolerance for those who are judgmental here. This approach to understanding bereavement is helping us to overcome the enormous inertia and stagnation that history has imprinted on our collective social awareness. Times are changing and our values with them, to our credit as a civilization. But this is happening slowly and not without great labor and pain.

Today, the deeply bereaved mourner for a beloved pet has some organized help available. At this writing, there are at least twenty-five centers across the United States where one may speak or meet with counselors who are experienced and trained for this specific problem. Most of them also offer wonderful group support sessions that are unmatched in the good they do for pet bereavement. Also, such help is usually free. These centers are listed at the end of this chapter. Some are telephone "hot lines" with specially selected and trained advisors.

As stated earlier, there is an amazing spectrum of counselors in this field, and their numbers are rapidly increasing. It is important to take warning, though. The newly bereaved are especially vulnerable and easily duped. There is always the presence of the few unscrupulous people who enter this field only for financial reward, without appropriate qualifications or experience. Others may love the sense of power and control that counseling offers them.

What Religion May Offer

We reach out for any help and guidance available. Unfortunately, there have been precious few responses from theology. Fundamental religions are not concerned with the death of companion animals. They are too rooted in tradition and the past. Their view is understandable since civilization in biblical times saw very few pets, and there was no need for such considerations. True pets were very rare luxuries and were usually kept only by royalty.

Certain Eastern philosophies and religions hold that all life is precious and intrinsically one and the same. It is part of the great unity of being. Thus the passing of a pet is respected as equal to that of a human. Here we can find a new perspective and solace in our bereavement for a pet. There is much to be considered and learned.

Islam, to its credit, respects the souls of all living things. But you will never see a dog in the home of a fundamentalist. The Koran, like the Old Testament, makes no reference at all to pets, since they were practically nonexistent. A strong general concern for the humane treatment of all animals is emphasized instead.

For thousands of years, Native Americans have revered life and spirit in all animals, even in those that they had to hunt. Although dogs roamed freely through the camps and belonged to no one, they were respected and treated almost like members of the tribe. It was believed that death took the dogs to the same "happy hunting grounds" that humans went to.

Unfortunately, most organized religions may not be able to help, since they are not philosophically or historically oriented in this specific direction. The rare exceptions lie with a few variant attitudes. In Christianity, St. Francis is the patron saint of animals and pets. Here, the individual priest has extreme latitude; no guidelines exist that define a firm position about whether pets have souls, go to heaven and so on. When offering solace to the person mourning for a pet, each cleric may deal with this as he wishes, in accordance with personal preference and practicality. The compassionate priest who is a real pet lover may be a fine counselor in pet bereavement. But that is only because of his unique personality and approach. He is too often an exception.

Take heart, however. Some major denominations are just beginning to follow the fine example of the Episcopal Cathedral Church of St. John the Divine, in New York City. They have set the modern standard for loving respect and consideration of pets and the effects their deaths have on us. Their very impressive annual St. Francis Day celebration is begun with a blessing of an amazing host of animals, and it is always a major feature on the television news of the day.

Death is a profoundly spiritual experience, and most people in pet bereavement feel a great need to turn to their spiritual leaders. But too often that kind of help is not sanctioned. Rather than appearing pessimistic when viewing the historical record of religion, a detailed study has been made for your consideration. The next chapter is designed to give a more in-depth perspective of the positive role that religion may still play in the life and death struggles of the grieving pet owner. Pastoral counseling, if available during the mourning period, can offer unique and very effective help and hope. But too often, it is difficult or impossible to find. A sense of spiritual uplift is particularly beneficial and often desired at this tragic time. Perhaps, by surveying some of the best contemporary religious thought concerning the death of pets, one may find some important insights and self-counsel.

Comfort in Philosophy

There is also consolation to be found in philosophy. Metaphysical philosophers and transcendental poets offer beautiful hope in this area. In addition to their other merits, they are well worth reading for this inspiration and incidental support

COUNSELING CENTERS AND HOT LINES

The Animal Medical Center
New York City
(212) 838-8100

ASPCA
New York City
(212) 876-7700

Bide-A-Wee Foundation
New York City
(212) 532-6395

CAAA Companion Animals Association of Arizona
Scottsdale, AZ
(602) 995–5885

University of California
School of Veterinary Medicine
Davis
(916) 752-4200

Chicago Veterinary Medical Association
Chicago
(708) 603-3994

Colorado State University
School of Veterinary Medicine
Fort Collins
(303) 221-4535

University of Florida
Gainsville
(352) 392-4700 ext. 4080

The Grief Recovery Institute
Beverly Hills, CA
(telephone hotline)
(888) 773-2683

Iowa State University
Pet Bereavement Hotline
(888) 478-7574

Michigan State University
School of Veterinary
Medicine
(517) 432-2696

University of Minnesota
School of Veterinary Medicine
Minneapolis
(612) 624-4747

University of Pennsylvania
School of Veterinary Medicine
Philadelphia
(215) 898-4525

Pet Friends, Inc.
Montclaire, NJ
(telephone hotline)
(800) 404-7387

St. Hubert's Giralda
Madison, NJ
(201) 377-7094

Tufts University
School of Veterinary
Medicine
Boston, Massachusetts
(508) 839-7996

College of Veterinary Medicine
Virginia-Maryland
(540) 231-8038

Washington State University
Pullman
(509) 335-4569

Note: There are several other listings for individuals or groups who are not associated with established institutions or organizations, and they are not listed here. Some of these have been found to represent only the personal, untrained approaches of the individuals in charge of them. Although others may be very fine, the above listing is only of authenticated institutions to date.

For a fee, other organizations such as the Delta Society compose listings of pet bereavement counselors, but there is no authentication of their verifiability as *bona fide* practitioners in this field.

Also, using your computer and modem, check the various online listings under "Pet Bereavement." There are many interesting services and chat rooms, as well as offerings for counseling and products. But it is always advisable to check the personal credentials of anyone claiming to be an authority or counselor in pet bereavement.

THE ASSOCIATION FOR PET LOSS AND BEREAVEMENT

The Association for Pet Loss and Bereavement is a confederation of diverse and concerned members who are experienced and knowledgeable in the area of pet death and its varying effects on those who acutely mourn this loss.

The purpose of this organization is to coordinate people who are suffering from pet bereavement with appropriate counseling, according to their individual needs. In serving as a clearinghouse for all pertinent information, the APLB prepares and publishes continually updated bibliographies and reports assessing all therapies and practitioners in this field.

The APLB recognizes that there are several controversial approaches to this type of counseling and that there are always some adherents who feel assured that these methods work for them. Although this association favors therapies based on more conventional counseling techniques for pet bereavement analysis and treatment, it registers anyone who conforms to reasonable standards of preparation and experience, regardless of methodology. It regularly upgrades that registry of practitioners with information on each counselor's background, training, experience and method of therapy. The APLB is continually open to suggestions, recommendations and petitions from additional individuals desiring to be included. It also offers special events such as occasional group support therapy sessions, publications and training seminars, as well as conferences open to the general public. At the time of this writing, it is the only approved organization to help teach and advise the pet bereavement counselor. Special training seminars are available to a variety of learners.

For more information about this outstanding organization and its activities, write or phone:

The Association for Pet Loss and Bereavement
P.O. Box 106
Brooklyn, NY 11230
(718) 382-0690
Internet address: www.aplb.org
E-mail address: aplb@aplb.org

Bless these pets, O Lord.   *Courtesy, Abbey Glen Pet Memorial Park*

CHAPTER 16

Religion
and the
Death
of Pets

A righteous man regardeth the life of his beasts.

—Prov. 7:10

*T*raditionally, our understanding of and preparation for death had been a subject that fell solely within the province of religion. With the exception of a few metaphysical philosophers, the clergy was the only acknowledged authority on the subject. Historically, however, since the Industrial Revolution our lifestyles have been changing dramatically, affecting this situation.

With the onset of the phenomenal growth in the size and population of cities, there came a corresponding decline in rural population. Partly as a result of this, there has been a gradual disappearance of the extended family and a diminishment of the traditionally powerful influence of organized religion on individuals. The previously unchallenged regulation of the church over everyday matters was strongly affected by the ever-changing socio-economic condition that prevailed.

The keeping of pets for pleasure and companionship had originally been the practice of nobility and landed gentry. As populations started to shift to the cities, basic lifestyles changed, and more people started discovering the satisfaction of having a personal pet. With the advent of increased wealth and leisure, this natural source of human pleasure began to gain popularity. Within the span of just a few hundred years, pet dogs and cats were seen everywhere. A graphic illustration of this is New York City. At the turn of the twentieth century, the population had only a few thousand pet dogs. Today there are well over one million, with even more cats. And who can begin to guess at the great numbers of other living things who are also being kept as pets? Of course, the human population has risen as well.

DO ANIMALS HAVE SOULS?

It was inevitable that the dramatic increase in the number of people with pets would result in a heightened public awareness of this relatively new historic phenomenon, the human-pet bond. Gradually, people began to enrich themselves through a close, personal relationship with a companion animal. But they quickly discovered that the pet's eventual death raised questions about whether such a sentient, loving animal also had a soul that would find its reward in heaven. In bereavement, it is often wondered, after our own deaths, if we will ever join our beloved pets again in some divine afterlife. The death of cherished animals presented a new problem, which had been ignored or scoffed at, at best, until very recently. Organized Western religion had no established authority or precedent for this. As a result, it was unable to offer solace to people mourning the death of their companion animals. The word "pet" is not mentioned in the Bible or New Testament. Reference is made only to animals in general, with instruction that they should be treated with humane care. In effect, religion turned its back on this evolving problem.

What Does the Bible Say?

Farm animals have always been common, even in biblical times, often sharing the same shelter as their masters. But the harsh demands of survival required that even the most lovable of these animals first serve their utilitarian functions. Many were raised for slaughter, others for milking. Certain animals, especially their adorable young, must have elicited affection and some special regard from their masters and their families. We find constant instruction in the Old Testament for the humane treatment of animals. But the concept of pets per se was still in the future, and the word "pet" did not yet exist. The first recorded use of that word was made at about A.D. 1000.

All religions with a basis in fundamental interpretation of the Bible have no literal criteria to deal with anything concerning the subject of pets. Despite biblical interest in the humane treatment of animals, the subject of a pet's death seemed unworthy of consideration. Even at this time there are many religious leaders who believe that only the life and death of humans should merit their involvement and concern. So where can the pet owner turn for spiritual help when a beloved animal dies?

Despite the historic novelty of this problem, genuine concern is growing among a few modern spiritual leaders. Humanistic responsibility demands that we care for each other when we are in deep distress. That caring now is extending to the legitimate, passionate question about the meaning of death for our pets, as well. Humans have a natural craving for some spiritual guidance and uplift. Some of our more modern religious leaders are taking strong notice of this and trying to do something positive.

What Religion Can Offer Us

It all boils down to this ultimate question: In this modern day, what can organized religion do to help deeply grieving pet owners? Many people have felt abandoned by their religion at this very critical time of their lives. They sought wisdom, solace and counsel from their source of traditional spiritual values, but they were left without any hope or help. Religious leaders could not offer anything better than generalizations. Where was love? Many of these bereaving individuals have turned away from their religion to some degree because they feel bitter and painful resentment. Despite whatever lay counsel can be offered, we can only treat the pain and suffering. A spiritual perspective, founded in religious ideology, is very often needed and sought.

When preparing this chapter, telephone calls and visits were made and letters were sent to leaders of the major religions of the world: Catholicism, Protestantism, Judaism, Buddhism and Islam. After a while it became evident that those faiths based upon a fundamentalist point of view felt that they had nothing to say about the problem and would not participate in this endeavor. It was also disappointing that the Catholic Archdiocese of New York suggested that this chapter be printed without their point of view because of their "time constraints." They didn't want to touch the issue.

The following is presented with much hope that the considerations offer some spiritual guidance and uplift.

THE JUDEO-CHRISTIAN PHILOSOPHY AND THE BUDDHIST VIEW

Judeo-Christian theology is based upon a God of love, who created all things lovingly. In Genesis it is established that we are to care for the rest of God's creations as stewards of the earth. He made a covenant with us to that effect. We are to have a loving relationship with all of His creations. We are obligated to treat the total world as lovingly as we can, as we know He does. That is part of our responsibility and what it means to be alive, here, created in God's image.

In the story of Noah we are told, "Behold, I establish my covenant with you, and your descendants after you, and with every living creature that is with you; the birds, the cattle and every beast of the earth with you. This is the sign of the covenant, which I make between Me and you and every living creature that is with you. For all future generations I set my rainbow in the cloud, and it shall be a sign of the covenant between me and the earth."

God's loving contract is not made exclusively with humans, but with all living creatures. There is a kind of equality established that we must take into account very seriously. After centuries of disregard, religion is slowly taking up the contemporary issue of man's struggle to better understand his bereavement for a beloved pet. Some modern spiritual leaders have offered us their thoughts on this.

THE JEWISH PERSPECTIVE

"While Judaism does not address itself specifically to the subject of the concern for or care of pets, it is deeply concerned about the humane treatment of all living things. In English, the principle would be called 'pain to living things.' Animals are a part of God's creation. Humanity has a responsibility to protect them, to avoid bringing unnecessary pain to them, and to treat them without cruelty. Thus, we find a biblical prohibition against plowing with an ox and an ass together (Deut. xxii, 10), on the assumption that the ox, being stronger, would bring pain to the ass. Sabbath laws of rest also apply to the animal kingdom (Exod. xx, 10; Deut. v, 14). From an application of humane consideration it is even forbidden to slaughter an animal and its young on the same day (Lev. xxii, 28). This same concern is exhibited in such biblical laws as the ones demanding that an animal struggling under too heavy a load have the burden removed (Exod. xxiii, 5), and releasing the parent bird from the nest before taking the young (Deut. xxii, 67). Indications of this same consideration for the welfare of animals can be seen in such narrative tales as when the angel rebuked Balaam for beating his beast, an ass (Num. xxii, 23), and when God chastised Jonah for not having compassion for the residents of Ninevah, 'that great city, wherein are more than six score thousand persons . . . and also much cattle' (Jonah iv, 11).

"The rabbinic tradition expanded on the biblical compassion for all living things. One of the seven Noachian Laws (laws that were to be observed universally, not just by Jews) prohibits the eating of the flesh of a living animal. While the rabbis were not opposed to the killing of animals for food, that act had to be performed with the greatest of compassion and speed. It was regulated with strict detail. It was forbidden for a man to eat before he had fed and tended to his animals, and it was out of this same consideration for their welfare that 'a man is not

permitted to buy animals unless he can properly provide for them.' The compassionate consideration for the welfare of animals, codified in Jewish law, also finds its expression in legendary material of the Jewish tradition. For example, it is said that Moses and David were considered fit to be leaders of Israel only after they had been shepherds.

"Out of this tradition, it is legitimate to extract an attitude of sympathetic response to the loss of a pet and to the tender administration of a pet's remains. A pet, having brought joy to the life of its owner, is as deserving of loving care in death as it was in its lifetime. However, after its death and disposal, one is not expected to mourn excessively or become involved in bizarre or unnecessarily expensive practices, any more than such expressions would be tolerated after the death of a person.

"Death is a part of life, and after death and reasonable mourning, life is to continue normally as quickly as possible."

Rabbi Balfour Brickner
Senior Rabbi Emeritus
The Stephen Wise Free Synagogue
New York City

HONORING A LOVING RELATIONSHIP

We should consider our personal reaffirmation of the relationship between God and creation. If we, alone, are given the particular gift to understand this, then we have the responsibility to help bring it about. We must care for all other living things, as well. When any part of creation dies, we must treat it as lovingly as the Creator would. Whenever there is a death in any loving relationship, it must be dealt with in a respectful manner. That is in honor of the loving relationship, which is also God's.

We know how it feels to grieve over the loss of something we love. God's love is demonstrated through us. It is godly to grieve over the loss of a pet because He grieves over the loss of any life.

Our grief is terrible enough without self-imposed guilt. The necessary taking of a pet's life, by euthanasia, can upset the religious harmony within some people. Despite the dire and demanding circumstances, it could be felt that God's commandment, "Thou shalt not kill," may have been taken in vain. But if the act is truly one of mercy and compassion, then God's love is expressed in this performance of duty, and the pet owner is absolved of sin and guilt.

This "mercy killing" falls into a special category, far from the otherwise sinful act of indifferent killing. We express God's love in preventing any further unavoidable pain and suffering and actually bestow a personal blessing on the pet. This is, in effect, an intense act of love. Indeed, it is God's love expressed through us in a very disturbing and extreme private sacrifice. We must wrap ourselves in the beauty and love of that life, keep it with us and go on as better humans because of it. It does, however, still cause us untold grief.

The Christian point of view emphasizes resurrection and the life that comes out of death. We are taught that the God of creation is always making new life and new relationships. But it is important not to get mired in our grief. We must allow the remembrance and understanding of that love to give birth to new opportunities for us to love. We can do this only when we travel through the valley of the shadow of death. We must come out of it. The grieving process must be lived through, from beginning to end. If not, we make trouble for our inner selves.

There is nothing in the scriptures that suggests that any living thing other than man has a soul. To wonder about this is a projection of our anthropomorphic fantasy; we are limited to our human perspective. But it must also be said that there is nothing in the scriptures that denies the existence of a soul for any other creature of creation. We are just not privy to God's larger view of truth. Things are not as obvious as they seem, and many important meanings are hidden.

Much of the Bible's wisdom is expressed in parables and metaphors. Wisdom is derived from a diligent search for their interpretations. The Creator made a covenant with the whole of the animal kingdom, including man as steward. There has always been a strong bond between many of us and our charges. We have come to know that there is a capacity for animals to love, and it is natural for us to wonder if they could possibly possess some spirituality unknown to us. One may easily conclude that there is some spiritual dimension to the life and death of other life forms in God's creation. But that would be a personal assumption.

THE HEREAFTER

Some say that when we think about meeting again in some after-life, it is based on a cognitive recognition that we enjoy in this life. The question of whether we will ever meet again in the hereafter aris-es out of our emotional involvement with grief and loss. In a sense, it is a fruitless question because the answer cannot be known to us. Aspiring to understand it is an attempt to fulfill an earthly need that may not be a need in whatever life there will be hereafter. But the human condition is one of passion, and this insatiable need to know is very important, as an afterthought of our love for our pets.

The answer could be truth for some future dimension of our exis-tence after death. We cannot possibly know it in this life. But we pose the question as a reflection of the grief and urgency of today. We must live through the period of grief and mourning, affirming its value for now. Whether one will ever see that pet again is not as important an issue as what one does with the love for and from that pet—and how that love has improved one's life. Ideally, such a profound experience should eventually help the bereaving pet owner. But in our minds, we tend to create hellish, as well as heavenly, conditions.

The church would affirm that the real question is how to accept and deal with the pain that comes from such a profound loss, result-ing from the love of a pet. A funeral is all about putting away the body, saying good-bye to the physical form and giving thanks for the spiritual. But since nothing is known about the spiritual dimensions of the animal kingdom, most religions do not officially sanction such services for them.

But there are many possible liturgies that can be used in the death of a pet, without getting involved with the affirmation of the spirit-ual. Pondering whether we will ever meet with the pet in the here-after just doesn't get any answers. That is a problem that can only be resolved by an individual and his or her own innermost sense of being.

We are so involved with trying to deal with our daily lives that going off into the much broader spectrum of the rest of creation can seem fruitless. It is something that most organized religions just have not found the necessity or the time to do.

St. Francis of Assisi (1182–1226) was a lover of creation. He felt that we are all part of nature and are interrelated. We are one with all of creation. He understood the Creator's love to encompass all living

156

things, including man. He believed that God, man and nature were all part of the same truth. Perhaps it was not such a coincidence that Christ was born in a manger, surrounded by animals. Nobody has ever given that any serious consideration. Possibly there is a profound metaphor and lesson in this.

SOME EPISCOPAL REFLECTIONS

"For people of faith, especially of the Judeo-Christian tradi-
tions, creation is the living act of a loving God. And for those
persons who have special relationships with various members of
the animal kingdom, it is important to understand the creatures
of this world, big and small, as wonderful manifestations of that
creative act. That which is before us, after us, above us, below
us, beyond us, within us; that Mother/Father of all life is called
by many different names, yet experienced by a majority of the
human beings of this earth as that one true origin of all life.
Plant, animal or human, no matter what the name of the child,
one must wonder if it is truly possible for the Mother/Father to
care more for one than another. Can the love of the Creator for
that which is created be unequally given? I think not, if I am to
trust my own feelings as a parent, and am a product of the
Creator's will. ('Let us make man in Our image.' Gen. i, 26.)

"The Judeo-Christian tradition leads me and many others to
believe in God's love for all living things. It also reminds people
of our role as stewards of that creation, of all living things.
Therefore, we are to act lovingly to all life, as would God.

"It is natural to grieve; it is the loss of that which is love.
Again and again, scripture reminds us that God grieved and still
grieves for that which is created when it is no longer truly alive.
So it is not only natural but right that, created in God's image,
we too grieve when life is lost, any life—all life. It is natural and
right to grieve over the loss of a pet that we loved, as God loves.
Would the God of love expect anything less of us? I think not.

"There are those who ask the question, 'Do animals have
souls like ours, and will they be with us in an afterlife?' In a loss
situation this question is best heard as an expression of the deep
love for that which is lost in death. It is not so important to
search for the answer to that which only God knows, as to trust

that which God loved is always under God's care. We, as a people of faith, are our own proof of this comforting truth."

Reverend Canon Joel A. Gibson
Subdean
The Cathedral Church of
St. John the Divine
New York City

A UNITARIAN-UNIVERSALIST PERSPECTIVE

"In the statement of Principles and Purposes of the Unitarian Universalist Association we affirm the inherent worth and dignity of every person, and the interdependent web of existence, of which we are a part.

"In the first of these two affirmations, Unitarian Universalism tells us that each one of us has the freedom to decide what is true and right for herself or himself, and the responsibility to act according to these beliefs. In the second we are reminded that what is true and right for each of us must take into account our place in the interdependent web. Both principles can guide us when we are with one who is grieving over the loss of a beloved pet.

"Humans and animals are part of this web—and it is a special strand of love and companionship that links pet and pet owner. Pets are important life companions. They take us out of ourselves by calling us to respond to them, watch them, engage with them. They demand of us responsibility, that we attend to their needs with care. They give to us joy in life, a different perspective, a relief from loneliness, along with their love.

"When that connecting strand is broken—when a pet dies — the resulting feelings of loss are real and significant. And, in that moment, we must attend to the brokenness, guided by the principle of inherent worth and dignity. The person who is grieving knows what the loss means for him or her. And this is the starting point. In our respect for them we can participate in acknowledging the reality of the loss, affirming the feelings of bereavement, of emptiness, in remembering the happy moments, and in learning to say good-bye.

"In the spirit of earth-centered religious traditions, we take time to honor and acknowledge our animal brothers and sisters with whom we share this planet. In the tradition of St. Francis we set aside a time to bless the animals who are part of our lives. We find ways to celebrate the intertwining of these strands of life. And so it is fitting that we also take time and find ways to mourn the loss and share the grief that the death of a pet brings."

—*Reverend Dr. Tracy Robinson-Harris*
Unitarian Universalist
Community Church of New York

Eastern philosophy and religious practice has always offered enriched perspectives to the traditional Western ways of looking at things. Although there are many differing sects in Buddhism, Zen being the best known, they all follow the basic teachings of Buddha—each with some variation. In its fascinating wisdom, the viewpoint offered here can offer hope to the bereaving pet owner. Not surprisingly, it is similar to the transcendental view of life, widely praised by American and British poets in the middle of the nineteenth century.

A BUDDHIST POINT OF VIEW

"According to the teachings of Mahayana Buddhism, the main goal of a practitioner is to lead all sentient beings to Supreme Freedom. This is an irreversible state which is free of all suffering and the causes of suffering. It is the state in which the Supreme Bliss is obtained.

"The wish to actually do this is called the altruistic thought of bodhicitta, and is the entrance to the Mahayana path of spiritual development. This altruistic thought has to be arrived at through preliminary practices. First, one meditates on equanimity, which is an antidote to being overly attached to friends—and adverse toward those we perceive as enemies. When one develops equanimity, one then meditates on what we believe is a fact, that all sentient beings have been our mother.

"There is no beginning to consciousness; this moment is a continuation of a previous moment of consciousness. Therefore, we all have undergone countless previous rebirths.

159

By this reasoning we can consider all sentient beings as having been our mothers—this applies as well to all animals, including cats and dogs. In their role as our mother they showed us great kindness. We can also observe how animal mothers display kindness in caring for their present offspring. We don't recognize them as our previous mothers because of our new life forms, but they have actually been our mothers, many times.

"Sentient beings are kind to us in all ways, not only in the role of mother. Therefore according to the Tibetan Buddhist tradition all sentient beings, including our domestic pets, deserve our kindness, in return. We must do our best to care for their needs and keep them happy and healthy.

"In Tibet it was a custom to purchase sheep and goats who were to be butchered, and then keep them as domestic animals. It was thought that saving the life of an animal was especially helpful when one was ill. Many Tibetans would walk with their animals around temples and holy shrines. Some temples would allow animals inside. Buddhists believe that it is beneficial for an animal to see a religious painting or image or to hear the sound of prayers and teachings. Hearing the sound of prayers and texts is thought to create the cause for an animal to obtain a favorable rebirth.

"When my own cat, 'Jack Benny,' had kidney problems, I bought a cassette recorder. I then played tapes of the teachings of His Holiness, the Dalai Lama, so the cat could hear them repeatedly over several days. I am not the only one who does this. Many people read their daily prayers loud enough for their pets to hear.

"When an animal is dying it is customary to recite the names of the Buddhas and Bodhisattvas to the animal. Hearing these names is especially helpful at the time of death. After the animal has died, holy people can be requested to pray for the deceased pet. One can also go to the temple and make offerings and pray for the animal.

"We believe that in the future all sentient beings can, and in fact will, attain the state of Buddhahood—the state of Supreme Freedom. This is possible because their consciousness is *separable from the defilements that currently prevent their attainment of this state. Therefore, every sentient being will become enlightened in the future, when they apply the techniques which separate defilements from their consciousness.*

"Of course, it is natural for an animal's owner to suffer and be unhappy over the death of a pet. But as I mentioned before, rather than just being unhappy, the owner can take positive actions to help him or herself and the pet. Say prayers for the pet; do religious practices and dedicate them to the pet. Many religious practitioners remember their deceased loved ones all the time in their daily prayers. They generate and maintain the wish to benefit them, and pray that they will be able to help them obtain better and better rebirths, better and better opportunities for spiritual development—and eventually highest enlightenment."

The Venerable Khyongla Rato Rinpoche
Tibet Center
New York

As the reader already well knows, there is no simple or single answer to our questions and grief. But the collected wisdom of the ages should be of assistance in our search for truths. This chapter is designed to lend some spiritual perspective to the bereaved person, regardless of what religion he or she elects to observe or not observe. One may well be an agnostic, yet believe that there is some sort of unnamed, all-pervading force within the cosmos. All of this offers hope, which is the balm and nourishment we need at this critical time. And hope is a great gift to us, which should be used to constantly improve our lives. Unfortunately, there are times when we give hope little or no attention. This diminishes us.

Whether we call it by the name religion or by any other word, our search for spiritual values and help is a prime force in our human existence on this plane. Each person's private odyssey in this search should be a mission integral to his or her self-respect and growth. If the viewpoints presented in this chapter offer some spiritual help in this search, then you are in a position to enrich your life, at least to that extent. The continuity of life is all around us. With hope and time we grow better and better in our own renewing lives.

ALL PETS GO TO HEAVEN

Can you imagine a heaven without pets?

There is a very special place where beloved pets go after they die. This is only a temporary location. But there are trees and grass and lakes and everything they love. Here they can play and eat and sleep, even better than they did before they died. Now there are no aches or worries or dangers of any kind to trouble or threaten them. The only joy missing is their beloved human companion, you.

All health is restored completely, and all injuries are healed. Dogs and cats play with each other like youngsters, and they do not have time to feel lonely for you. They miss you, but with the special wisdom that animals have, they trust that this condition will get better. And they confidently wait as they frolic.

A wonderful day will come for each of them, when in the middle of playing, they will suddenly feel something is different. And all their senses will be at the height of excitement and exuberance. They will sniff the air and look off in the distance where they recognize that dearly loved, very special presence. Then they will call out in elation and, with eyes shining and tail going wild, tear off at a full gallop, almost flying over the green grass.

Your expected arrival has been sensed, and now there is nothing that can keep the two of you apart ever again. As you run toward each other, the tears jump from your eyes. Your pet leaps into your arms, and you cling together in jubilant reunion. The joyous kisses rain on your face, and you kiss back just as ecstatically. Your hands so lovingly caress once more the beloved fur, the head and neck and body you knew so well. And you look into each other's loving eyes and know that now everything is put aright.

And then something will call the both of you on to a different field of warmth and nurture, where all the love you knew now comes to fruition. With your pet, you leave that special waiting area, pass into the main part of heaven and begin a new existence there, together.

If you accept that pets can love us as much as we love them, then the logic is clear and cannot be denied. If you believe that there is a heaven for people, then they must be there, waiting for us, when we cross over. Heaven is love, and pets always share that with us.

CHAPTER 17

Some Practical Suggestions in Review

Build thee more stately mansions, O my soul!

—Oliver Wendell Holmes

*I*n concluding this book, it is thought advisable to list some practical suggestions that have been gleaned over years of experience with pet bereavement. Not all of them may seem right or timely for you, but most of them will. Whatever you choose to do at this time of extreme heartache is very private and not to be judged by anyone else. The only thing that should be criticized is inaction to help yourself. Your pet would have wanted you to heal yourself as quickly as you could. These suggestions will help you do that:

1. Let your feelings out. Cry. Don't hold back. Your emotion has to come out. The pain and confusion will start to get sorted out. If you suppress your feelings, it will only delay

In memory of all those who have gone before us and remain in our hearts and minds.

Courtesy, Hartsdale Canine Cemetery, Inc.

the healing and mourning processes. Sometimes it is advisable to allow yourself some sort of indulgence to loosen up, possibly a little wine or other spirit, and to drink a toast to your beloved pet and its memory. Share this with others, but don't get oppressive.

2. Write a letter or will from your pet to yourself. Keep this as a permanent memory. You may be amazed at how much this reveals to you about yourself. Years later this will become a very valuable personal document.

3. Dedicate something in your pet's name and memory. Donations to worthy causes are good. Usually gifts that require a plaque or permanent label give great satisfaction. If your pet was a show animal, then donating a memorial trophy to a pet club is very gratifying. Most humane organizations will appreciate a donation in your pet's name and memory.

4. It is not too late to say something to your deceased pet. Over a period of time, make a list of all the loving memories you have of your pet. Constantly amend this list. Then write a letter to your pet, remembering all these intimate smiles and tears. Keep this as part of your loving good-bye in this life. But remember, the loving memories live on forever with you, so something of your beloved pet will never die and leave you. Letting go of the pain does not mean that you are letting go of the loving memories. This list and letter will take on added value with time.

5. Make an audio recording of yourself, reading these memories and saying whatever emotional, private things you feel. Listen to it a few times during your mourning, and add to it whenever it feels right. Keep this as a permanent part of your personal memorial to your beloved pet. You may be surprised at how effective this is when you play it back years later. It will become precious as time goes on.

6. Establish new routines. Change or vary the old ones. (We fall into the usual emotional responses when we follow old patterns.) Deliberately do things in a changed order as soon as you get up in the morning. At home, try sitting in

165

a different chair or place on the couch. Rearrange your furniture. Work, shop, meditate, attend social functions, walk, jog, run, bike and partake in special events, sports or concerts with other people. Most importantly, start meeting with people again. Avoid being alone too often. Attend pet bereavement support groups. Regular exercise helps reduce depression, and it helps promote emotional healing.

7. Invite friends, relatives or good neighbors to visit you in your home. Visit other pet owners and their pets. Return (with company?) to some of the sites you shared with your pet. This will help you accept how separate the past is from the present. Embrace closure with your loving memories. You can keep your remembrances without their fading in the future. As time goes on, they become even more enriched.

8. Treat yourself to things you would have liked, but couldn't or wouldn't do before. Imagine your pet's spirit advising you how to ease your pain. Do some enjoyable things with your pet's blessings. Certainly you deserve them. As soon as you can, go on a trip or vacation. If it appealed to you before, now is the right time to seriously consider relocating or changing your job.

9. Avoid keeping visible reminders of your grief. Get rid of your pet's toys and other things you may have wanted to keep as mementos. They are mostly painful and not good for you at this time. If you cannot throw them out yet, then put them out of sight in a drawer or a box in a closet or basement. The real memory is in your heart. You don't want to have to rely on items to remind you of your love and years together.

Don't make it harder for yourself to recover. Embrace your memories and strong feelings. Share them with people who understand, but don't get morbid. Go to pet bereavement group support sessions and tell your feelings to others who are undergoing the same misery. When you feel their tears, you will realize you are not alone.

166

10. As soon as you can, talk to your veterinarian. Make a list, in advance, of any questions or doubts you may have about your pet's death. This will prevent you from forgetting items while you are experiencing strong emotions. It should clear up any possible doubts about everything.

    Such a meeting should be warm and informational. Do not abuse it as a means to vent anger at your pet's doctor. Ask his or her advice about any special problems or questions that have been bothering you. Veterinarians have had considerable experience with other clients who have been through this. They may be able to offer you some practical information. Usually, most veterinarians try to stay clear of individual bereavements unless they are asked for advice. Keep in mind, however, that a vet is an authority, but not a trained counselor.

11. Unless there is an emergency, avoid the administration of euthanasia on special calendar dates such as birthdays or anniversaries. This could be upsetting in the future. Prevent yourself from linking unhappy associations with happy ones.

12. Understand and respect your own mourning. If your grief is intense, take some time off from work. Tell your employer that there has been a death in your immediate family. This certainly is true. Most employers provide a specific brief leave for this. Don't try to explain or give excuses. Even if you are prodded to say who died, you don't have to tell. Just say it is very personal, and walk away. Be firm and insistent, but not confrontational. Assert yourself at this time. You deserve it. If you cannot get any time off, at least you tried. If you still really feel you need it, take the time off without pay. Most likely, you will be respected for this, not criticized. But that may not always be the case at your place of employment.

13. When you are ready, visit an animal shelter to look around, not to adopt. You have to be firm with yourself about this. It will help you in many ways if you write down your feelings after this visit and read them again later.

What new thoughts are stimulated by this visit? Don't give in to any sudden impulses to adopt any of the animals you see there. If such a response remains with you, go back a second time and see if you still feel that way. With such feelings, maybe the time is now right.

14. Hold some sort of private service for your beloved pet. You will have wonderful, permanent memories of this. Only friends and family who would appreciate such a ceremony should be invited. Children definitely should be helped to feel they are a basic part of the family in planning and carrying out such a ceremony. This is a very positive activity that has proven to be one of the healthiest beginnings of the mourning process. A private service will help you understand your underlying feelings, with a dignity and pride you probably couldn't have appreciated before. It need not be of any traditional religious nature. Its purpose is to express your personal spiritual values in a loving retrospective. Be careful not to invite anyone who is not very sympathetic to your mourning. If you like, a few words from some of those people present, followed by your eulogy, should be sufficient—that is up to you. This will almost assuredly help you through the worst parts of your grief and healing process. Such a ceremony will enrich you and your loving memories.

15. Keep a daily log or journal. List your major thoughts and feelings, but keep it brief. If you feel that you want to write at length on the subject, do it separately. Perhaps that could be the basis for an interesting magazine article, essay or short story. Once each day's log is entered, don't change anything. Such a journal will become a treasured part of your memorial to your pet. It will also be of great personal value to you in gaining insight and objectivity into your own thoughts and feelings. (Reading parts of it might just offer hope and comfort to others, as well.)

16. Make a list of the things your pet did that used to make you laugh or smile. Add to it as often as you can, even if it takes weeks. Review the items. When you can share these good memories, laughs and tears, read the list to someone

who knew the pet and has been supportive during your mourning.

This is part of your healing. It is good medicine. Despite many tears, you will be happier and stronger after each reading of the list. Put it away and keep it forever, along with photographs and other memorabilia. In the future, you will treasure reading these precious memories.

17. Don't live the life of a hermit or of one who is atoning. Get out of the house. Go to a movie or museum. Turn on the television, instead of sitting in a silent room. Expose yourself to distractions and possible pleasure again. This is life. You deserve it.

These suggestions can be of great assistance for helping yourself. Be assured that from the very start of your bereavement, your love and tender memories will live on with you. The pain will diminish as a sense of closure starts to transform it into cherished memories. In letting go of one thing, you are reaching out and grasping something else that is very precious. And that is something that will never go away.

Kitten Mummy: Egyptian, Ptolemaic-Roman; Linen; Height: 20.5 cm., Width: 4.5 cm., Max depth: 6 cm. *Hay Collection, gift of Granville Way, courtesy, Museum of Fine Arts, Boston*

Resources

But if the while I think on thee, dear friend,
All losses are restored and sorrows end.

—*"Sonnets," John Milton*

PET CEMETERIES, CREMATORIES
AND FUNERAL PARLORS

There are many pet cemeteries, crematories and funeral parlors, and it is logical that they have formed specialized professional associations to represent themselves. While not all of these individual businesses are associated in this way, most are, and they are listed here for your convenience. It may also be advisable to look in your local Yellow Pages under "Pet Cemeteries," or other similar listings.

In these three listings, the size of the first organization is indicative of only its longer time in existence. The remaining two organizations have only recently emerged with much stricter professional rules and regulations for their members. When choosing a cemetery or crematory, the following lists are only offered as general guides. It is essential for the prospective client to make a reasonable analysis and inspection of the property, operation and legal protections that should be available. It is strongly advised to do this first to avoid any possible disappointments later. This is the last thing we do for a beloved pet, and it must be done right.

INTERNATIONAL ASSOCIATION OF PET CEMETERIES (IAPC)

"How a community honors its deceased companion animals is a strong indication of what kind of people live there. When selecting a pet funeral home or cemetery one can be assured that members of the International Association of Pet Cemeteries are dedicated to assisting those people who have strong feelings toward animals, in selecting the appropriate method of honoring a deceased pet. We take pride in assuring that this is done in a professional and caring manner."

Peter E. Drown, Executive Director
International Association of Pet Cemeteries

NAME	ADDRESS
AA Sorrento Valley Pet Cemetery	10801 Sorrento Valley Road San Diego, CA 92121
AAA Dog & Cat Cemetery	25280 Pennsylvania Road Taylor, MI 48180
Abbington Hill Pet Cemetery	148 Youngblood Road Montgomery, NY 12549
AFF Bill Halfpenny	1-5475 Lakeshore Road Burlington, Ont, Canada L7L 1 El
AFF Boone County Humane Society	228 West 16th Street Boone, IA 50036
AFF Dennis D Woodruff, D.V.M	4318 SE Army Post Road Des Moines, IA 50320
AFF Dr. Thomas Nicholl	9700 SW Kanner Highway Indiantown, FL 34956
AFF Gary D. Strassburg	P.O. Box 236 Niagara Falls, NY 14304

NAME	ADDRESS
AFF John A. Dudzinski	8758 Hillside Road Pickeft, WI 54964
AFF Laurie Dayhoff	1220 Winifred Drive Tallahassee, FL 32308
AFF Mickey Bassford	101 Rainbow Drive, Apt 7265 Livingston, TX 77351
AFF Pet Memories	618 235th Street Tipton, IA 52772
Affiliate	Box 3413, 2930 Harvard Avenue Butte, MT 59702
Alabama Pet Cemetery	P.O. Box 530217 Birmingham, AL 35253
All Creatures Memorial Gardens	23098 Hwy 1088 Mandeville, LA 70448
All Pets Go to Heaven Funeral Home	236 Carroll Street Brooklyn, NY 11231
Anderson Acres	12810 Foust Road Conneaut Lake, PA 16316
Angel Paws	24 Kimble Avenue Los Gatos, CA 95032
Angel Refuge Pet Cemetery	2726 Park Avenue West Ontario, OH 44906
Angel View Pet Cemetery	465 Wareham Street Middleboro, MA 02346
Asahi Pet Cemetery	150-1, Shigemitsu, Tobe-Cho Iyo-gun, Ehime, Japan 791-21
Atlanta Pet Cemetery & Crematory	P.O. Box 723694 Atlanta, GA 31139
Balmoral Pet Cemetery	P.O. Box 154, 744 Kent Road Gaylordsville, CT 06755

NAME	ADDRESS
Blueberry Ridge	RR #1, P.O. Box 252 East Eddington, ME 04428
Brookside Pet Cemetery	P.O. Box 67 York, PA 17405
Broward Pet Cemetery	11455 NW 8th Street Plantation, FL 33325
Bubbling Well Pet Memorial Park	2462 Atlas Peak Road Napa, CA 94558
Cape Pet Cemetery	125 NE Pine Island Road Cape Coral, FL 33909
Chestnut Ridge Pet Cemetery	RD #I, Box 630 Blairsville, PA 15717
City of Carson City	3770 Butti Way Carson City, NV 89701
Coldren Crates Funeral Home	205 West Sandusky Street Findlay, OH 45840
Companion Green Pet Cemetery	P.O. Box 127, Barton Road West Burke, VT 05871
Country Club Pet Memorial Park	624 147th Avenue SW Calgary, Alberta, Canada T2Y2E7
Country Meadows Pet Cemetery	11400 Dimondale Dimondale, MI 48821
Denver Pet Cemetery	57221 East 72nd Avenue Commerce City, CO 80022
Devonshire Pet Memorial Services	34 Regent Street St Johns, NF, Canada A1A 5C4
Dixie Memorial Pet Cemetery	7960 Epperson Mill Road Millington, TN 38053
Domestic Animal Cremation	Box 159 Headingley, Canada ROHOJO

NAME	ADDRESS
Driftwood Pet Memorial Gardens	P.O. Box 668, 800 East Laurel Road Laurel, FL 34272
Drownwood Forest Pet Cemetery	Box 163, 13 Cemetery Lane Ellenburg Depot, NY 12935
Dulaney Pet Haven	200 East Padonia Road Timonium, MD 21093
Eternal Love Pet Cemetery	94 Hickory Lane Bethlehem, CT 06751
Evergreen Memorial Park, Inc.	28624 North Turkey Creek Road Evergreen, CO 80439
Faithful Companion Pet Memorial Park	568 Violet Avenue Hyde Park, NY 12538
Faithful Companions Pet Cemetery	IRD 2, Box 210 Ulster, PA 18850
Faithful Friends Pet Cemetery	6217 Memorial Drive Sanston, VA 23150
Faithful Friends Pet Cemetery & Crematory	P.O. Box 16234 Forth Worth, TX 76133
Faithful Friends Pet Memorial	Service 18 Old Kings Road Sydney, Nova Scotia, Canada Bl S 2B5
Faithful Pets Memorial Gardens	RD #6, Box 446 Uniontown, PA 15401
Fawnwoods of Windridge Memorial	P.O. Box 459 Cary, IL 60013
Final Paws	356B Ridge Circle Drive Grand Junction, CO 81503
Forest Rest Memorial Park	2811 Hebron Avenue Glastonbury, CT 06033
Forever Friends Pet Cemetery	P.O. Box 761 Tea, SD 57064

NAME	ADDRESS
Forrest Run Pet Cemetery	W5123 Natures Way Sherwood, WI 54169
Franklin Pet Cemetery	2405 Ashby Road Merced, CA 95340
Friendship Pet Memorial Park	P.O. Box 265 Waldorf, MD 20604
Garden of Love Memorial Park	4421 North West 14th Place Gainesville, FL 32605
Gateway Pet Memorial Services	180 Southgate Drive Unit 3 Guelph, Ontario, Canada N1G 4P5
God's Creatures Pet Cemetery	11307 China Spring Road Waco, TX 76708
Great Valley Pet Cemetery	P.O. Box 805 Frazer, PA 19355
Greenbrier Memory Gardens for Pets	3703 West Kelly Park Road Apopka, FL 32712
Greenleaf Gardens	2510 Grand Boulevard, Box 01401 Kansas City, MO 64108
Harperlawn Pet Memorial Gardens	26600 Steamwood Lane Southfield, MI 48034
Harthaven Pet Crematory	P.O. Box 23-0227 Anchorage, AK 99523
Hartsdale Pet Cemetery	75 North Central Avenue Hartsdale, NY 10530
Hearthside Rest Pet Cemetery	3024 West 26th Street Erie, PA 16506
Herr Funeral Homes	510 West Main Collinsville, IL 62234
Hinsdale Animal Cemetery	6400 South Bentley Avenue Willowbrook, IL 60514

Name	Address
Humane Society of Rochester	99 Victor Road, P.O. Box 299 Fairport, NY 14450
Jancy Pet Cemetery	P.O. Box 870 Zellwood, FL 32798
Joto Pet Cemetery	5.16, Shirokanedai 5-Chome, St Tokyo, Japan 108
Kamik Memorial Gardens	5411 Black Road Waterville, OH 43566
Keystone Memorial Park	Rte. 42, Cheshire Road Bethany, CT 06524
Kimberly Memorial Park	P.O. Box 343 Fogelsville, PA 18051
Kozy Acres Pet Cemetery	18155 South Farrell Road Joliet, IL 60432
Lacey Memorial Pet Cemetery	R1OOO South Church Street Hazleton, PA 18201
Lake View Memorial Park	2786 Algoma Boulevard Oshkosh, WI 54901
Lap Pet Cemetery	Rt. 2 Box 78 AD Carrollton, MS 38917
Little Bit of Heaven	8726 Congo Lane Houston, TX 77040
Los Angeles Pet Memorial Park	P.O. Box 8517 Calabasas, CA 91302
Loving Rest Pet Cemetery	7308 Benton Drive Urbandale, IA 50322
Lynn Andrew	HC 3 Box 579 Payson, AZ 85541
Memory Gardens Cemetery for Pets	9055 Pendleton Pike Indianapolis, IN 46236

NAME	ADDRESS
Memory Gardens for Pets	1081 Dogwood Hill Watkinsville, GA 30677
Memory's Garden	1207 Greenwich Drive Albany, NY 12203
Midlands Pet Care, Inc.	P.O. Box 1846 Lexington, SC 29071
My Pet Memorial Park	10100 Church Road Utica, NY 13502
My Pet's Cemetery	430 Magnolia Avenue Petuma, CA 94952
Noah's Ark Pet Cemetery	7400 Lee Highway Falls Church, VA 22042
Noah's Gardens Pet Cemetery/Mortuary	2727 Orange Avenue, S.E. Grand Rapids, MI 49546
Oakrest Pet Gardens	4991 Peachtree Road Chamblee, GA 30341
Oldis Co., Ltd.	91-3 Vemadskogo Pr. Moscow, Russia 117602
Pals, Inc.	3829 North 40th Avenue Glendale, AZ 85019
Paw Print Gardens	27 West 150 North Avenue West Chicago, IL 60185
Paws Awhile Pet Memorial Park	3426 Brush Road Richfield, OH 44288
Paws in Heaven	HC 3 Box 7553J Canyon Lake, TX 78132
Peaceful Hills Pet Cemetery	5059 Highway K Hartford, WI 53027
Peaceful Pets Cemetery	1325 Mackey Ferry Road Mount Vernon, IN 47620

NAME	ADDRESS
Peaceful Pines Pet Memorial Park	188 Lois Lane Mosinee, WI 54455
Pennsylvania SPCA	Rt. 6, Rd. 7, Box 226 Wellsboro, PA 16901
Pet Cremation Services	3109 Denver Avenue Columbus, OH 43209
Pet Crematory Agency, Inc.	184 Cabot Street West Babylon, NY 11704
Pet Friend Ooita Co.	8.1, Tanaksmachi, Oaita-shi Ooita, Japan 870
Pet Grief Support Service	Scottsdale, AZ
Pet Haven Cemetery	4501-3 West Seneca Turnpike Syracuse, NY 13215
Pet Haven Cemetery	P.O. Box 572 Union Bridge, MD 21791
Pet Haven Cemetery, Inc.	23646 Military Road, Box 1147 Kent, WA 98035
Pet Heaven Memorial Park, Inc.	10901 Flagler Street Miami, FL 33174
Pet Land Memorial Park	5720 East Glenn Street Tucson, AZ 85712
Pet Lawn Memorial Park	Route 73, P.O. Box 22 Beriin, NJ 08009
Pet Memorial Cemetery	7704 Stonegate Lawton, OK 73505
Pet Paradisc, Inc.	4526 Office Park Drive, Suite 7 Jackson, MS 39206
Pet Rest Cemetery & Cremation Services	139 Alston Circle Goose Creek, SC 29445

NAME	ADDRESS
Pet Rest Gardens	7185 Gilleft Road Flushing, MI 08050
Pet Rest Memorial Park	RD 3, Box 464 Watsonville, PA 17777
Pet's Rest Cemetery	1905 Hillside Boulevard Colma, CA 94014
Petland Cemetery & Funeral Home	1155 East Wheat Road Vineland, NJ 08360
Pinellas Memorial Pet Cemetery	6505 85th Avenue North Pinellas Park, FL 34665
Precious Pets Cemetery	P.O. Box 300 Spencer, OK 73084
Rainbow Bridge Pet Aftercare	P.O. Box 338 Beaufort, SC 29901
Resthaven Memorial Gardens, Inc.	7401 US Rt. 15N, P.O. Box ISO Fredrick, MD 21701
Rolling Acres Complex	400 South 134th Street Lincoln, NE 68520
Rolling Hills Pet Cemetery	503 North Ann Boulevard Harkers Heights, TX 76543
Rome Pet Cemetery	21977 St. Rt. 243 Apt. B1 Proctorville, OH 45669
Rush Inter Pet Cemetery & Crematory	139 Rush Road West Rush, NY 14543
Saint Francis Columbarium Guild	P.O. Box 24125 Greenville, SC 29616
San Diego Pet Memorial Park	8985 Crestmar Point San Diego, CA 92121
Sandy Ridge Pet Cemetery	RR #1 Eden, Ontario, Canada NOJL HO

NAME	ADDRESS
Saratoga Springs Pet Cemetery	Rt. 9, Box 320 Saratoga Springs, NY 12868
Savannah Pet Cemetery	9 Salt Creek Road Savannah, GA 31405
Sierra Hills Pet Cemetery	6700 Verner Avenue Sacramento, CA 95841
Sugarloaf Pet Gardens	21511 Peach Tree Road, Box 415 Barnesville, MD 20838
Sunland Pet Rest	10917 Sunland Drive Sun City, AZ 85351
Sweet Dreams Pet Cemetery & Crematory	P.O. Box 167 Amelia, VA 23002
The Animal Memorial Cemetery	St Mary's Road, Berkshire Park New So. Wales, Australia 2765
The Farm Pet Cemetery	2375 North New Salem Road Salem, IN 47167
The Surrey Pet Cemetery & Crematory	Byers Lane South, Godstone Surrey, England RH9 8JL
Tokyo Memorial Co.	7-9, Asakusabashi 4- Chome Taito-ku, Tokyo, Japan 11
Toothacres Pet Care Center	1639 Parker Road Carrolton, TX 75008
Trail's End Pet Crematory	706 Horse Hill Road Westbrook, CT 06498
Tully's Pet Cemetery	338 North 130th Street Omaha, NE 68154
Union Cemetery Association	16301 North State Road 3N Eaton, IN 47338
Until We Meet Again Pet Services	Raymond Road Newington, Ont, Canada KOC 1YO

NAME	ADDRESS
Valley of the Temples Pet Memorial	47-200 Kahekill Highway Kaneohe, HI 96744
Valley Pet Cemetery	127 Britner Avenue Williamsport, MD 21795
Western Farm Pet Crematory & Cemetery	12521 South Island Road Grafton, OH 4404
Woodside Pet Cemetery	6450 Shepler Church Road, SW Navarre, OH 44662

ACCREDITED PET CEMETERY SOCIETY (APCS)

"This is a young organization and its numbers are just starting to increase. Strict requirements of membership and operation are established to protect the client and the pet's remains. Each member of this society must offer proof of quality and protection of service. This is accomplished through requirements of minimum acreage, as well as deed restrictions, covenants or other local means set forth by local laws to insure perpetuation of the pet cemetery. In addition to a long list of additional membership criteria, legal guarantees are also mandatory to insure quality permanent care of each cemetery. It is felt that the public should be able to expect certain basic assurances when choosing a pet cemetery or crematory. This organization is founded on that principle, and will admit only new members who are committed to this kind of excellence."

Polly Hanna, President
Accredited Pet Cemetery Society

NAME	ADDRESS
Abbey Glen Pet Memorial Park	187 Route 94 Lafayette, NJ 07848
Hartsdale Pet Cemetery	75 North Central Avenue Hartsdale, NY 10530
Paws Awhile Pet Memorial Park	3430 Brush Road Richfield, OH 44286
Pet Lawn Memorial Park	Route 73, P.O. Box 22 Berlin, NJ 08009
Pine Rest Pet Cemetery	757 Seneca Creek Road West Seneca, NY 14224
Pines Pet Cemetery	764 Riley Wills Road Lebanon, OH 45036
Rolling Acres Memorial Gardens for Pets	P.O. Box 12073 Kansas City, MO 64152
Rush Inter Pet Cemetery	139 Rush Road West Rush, NY 14543

NATIONAL ASSOCIATION OF PET FUNERAL DIRECTORS (NAPFD)

"The NAPFD is a relatively small and new association of pet cemetery/crematory/funeral directors, joining together to standardize service delivery, endorse prudent legislation and elevate the professional status of this industry and its specialists. In starting out new, we are able to require that each of our members is held to very high standards of excellence. Each member must maintain full compliance with our constitution, and undergo periodic evaluative inspections, satisfying our

high standards of operation. We are committed to a special responsibility with each grieving pet owner, and intend to provide the best possible professional service to commemorate the life and death of every beloved pet. Our growing reputation is our best advertisement."

Robin Lauder, President
National Association of Pet Funeral Directors

Name	Address
Abendblum Crematory	506 Boyds Corner Road, P.O. Box 195 Middletown, DE 19709
Forever Friends Pet Memorial Park	12810 Foust Road Conneaut Lake, PA 16316
Golden Lake Pet Memorial Gardens	210 Andersontown Road Mechanicsburg, PA 17055
Hinsdale Animal Cemetery	6400 South Bentley Avenue Clarendon Hills, IL 60514
Kozy Acres Pet Cemetery	18155 South Farrell Road Joliet, IL 60432
Oak Crest Pet Cemetery & Crematory	2845 Oakcrest Place Land O' Lakes, FL 34639
Penninsula Pet Rest	216 Longmeadow Drive Newport News, VA 23601
Pleasant Mountain Pet Rest & Crematory	76 Liberty Street Plymouth, MA 02360
Plumtree Pet Services	321 Jaywood Road Williston, SC 29853
Plumtree Pet Services	P.O. Box 387 Green Cove Springs, FL 32043

Glossary of Terms

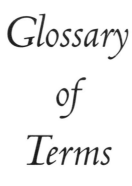

ABERRATION—Deviation from normal mental activity or from some standard of what is right or correct.

ALIENATION—Disappointment, leading to withdrawal or detachment of affection or feelings.

ANTHROPOMORPHIZE—To assign human characteristics to non-human things.

APATHY—The absence or lack of feeling, emotion or caring.

ARRESTED—Stopped, halted progress of normal functioning.

BATTERED—Subjected to strong or overwhelming attack, not necessarily physical.

BEREAVEMENT—The emotional state of being deprived of a loved one because of death.

BLOCK OUT—To be unable to recall something because of related emotional stress.

BONDING—Emotional attachment.

CLOSURE—The final stage of bereavement (resolution). The ability to be finally comfortable with a former major problem.

COLUMBARIUM (OSSUARY)—A vault or special repository for storing the ashes of cremated bodies.

COMPENSATE—To make amends, an adjustment, or supply an equivalent need.

CONDITIONED—Developed or modified by frequent usage or practice.

CONSTRUCT (n)—An object of thought created by the ordering or systematic uniting of elements. An intellectual or logical construction or operational concept.

CREMAINS—The ashes of a body after cremation.

DEFENSE MECHANISM—A psychological reaction in which one defends oneself emotionally.

DEPRESSION—A mental state characterized by very low spirits, sadness and feelings of inadequacy.

DYSFUNCTION—Impaired or abnormal functioning.

ETHOLOGIST—A person who studies the behavior of animals.

EUPHEMISM—The substitution of an agreeable word or phrase for one that is unpleasant.

EVOLVED—Gradually changed or transformed for the better; adapted over a period of time to progressive development or evolution.

EXISTENTIAL—Dealing with existence and being.

FALLIBLE—Capable of error or misperception.

FANTASY—A pleasant mental image created by the imagination to satisfy some need.

GUT FEELING—An extremely subjective, intuitive, personal response or appraisal lacking suitable explanation, yet profound in its effect on an individual.

HUMANE—An attitude marked by compassion, sympathy and consideration for other beings.

HUMANIST—A person marked by compassion, respect and strong interest in others.

INHERENT—Belonging by nature or settled habit.

JUDGMENTAL—Of or relating to judgment or criticism arising from a personal point of view.

JUSTIFICATION—Vindication or proof of usefulness; explanation or grounds for defending an action or behavior.

MAUDLIN—Gloomily tearful; miserable or excessively sentimental.

METAMORPHOSIS—A stage of growth in transition to higher development.

METAPHOR—A word or phrase used to imply a comparison or separate concept.

MIND-SET—An attitude of being close-minded, opinionated, or having a preconceived set of ideas or views on a subject.

MISPERCEPTION—The incorrect understanding or seeing of an idea.

MORBIDITY—A state of intense misery, discomfort and pain, resulting from disease or upset.

MORES—The morally binding customs or traditions of an established society.

MORTALITY—Fatality caused by a disease, drug or action.

MORTUARY—A business dealing with death and burial.

NEUROTIC—Describing a personal pattern of behavior caused by conflict and insecurity and marked by tension.

OBJECTIVE (adj)—Clear; able to make an independent appraisal of an idea or situation without being affected by personal feelings or prejudices.

OBSESSIVE—Excessive in some interest or repeated action, sometimes to the point of abnormality.

OSSUARY (COLUMBARIUM)—A vault or receptacle for the bones/ashes of the dead.

PARADOXICAL—At first, seemingly contradictory or opposed to logic, yet valid.

PATHOLOGICAL—Unhealthy; damaging to physical or mental well-being.

PERCEPTION—Individual awareness or intuitive recognition, insight or intellectual grasp.

PERSPECTIVE—A view of a whole entity in relation and proportion to all its parts.

PLACEBO EFFECT—Physical or psychological reaction caused by presumption that a specific medicine or treatment will have its effect, regardless of its capability. (This demonstrates unconscious mind over body control, allowing counterfeit remedies to be effective if they are believed to be real.)

POST-TRAUMATIC STRESS—Exceptional stress that is caused by a severe emotional shock.

PROGNOSIS—The foretelling of how a condition or disease will change over time.

REPRESS—To deliberately try to exclude from conscious awareness.

ROLE MODEL—A person one looks up to and imitates.

SECONDARY ANGER—The release of pent-up anger, which is triggered by a completely different stimulus not meriting this response.

SELF-DEFEATISM—The act of defeating one's own purposes by unconsciously sabotaging what is thought or done.

SELF-RECRIMINATION—The act of accusing or blaming one's self.

SENTIENT—Aware; consciously perceiving, thinking, feeling.

SEPARATION ANXIETY—Anxiety or distress caused by death or separation.

SLAUGHTERHOUSE REFORM—Social reform to pass laws to remedy the horrible and inhumane conditions in slaughterhouses.

STIMULI—Things that rouse the body, mind or feelings.

SUBCONSCIOUS—The function of the brain in which mental processes take place just below an immediate level of awareness.

SUBJECTIVE—Describing a particular individual's perception, which is modified by personal bias and limitations.

SUPPRESS—To unconsciously or subconsciously impede or inhibit from conscious thought or feeling.

SURROGATE—A substitute, or one appointed to act for another.

SYMBIOTIC—The positive mutual relationship of two dissimilar organisms, in which each helps the other in some way.

SYMBOL—Anything that suggests or associates other things or ideas.

SYNDROME—A group of related symptoms, collectively typical of a particular problem.

TACTILE CONTACT—Physical contact by touching and feeling.

THERAPEUTIC—Having to do with remedial treatment of a disease.

TRANSCENDENCE—The going beyond usual spiritual limits; excelling, surpassing.

TRAUMA—A state or condition of physical, mental or emotional shock, produced by extreme stress or injury. Emotional stress or blow that may produce disordered feelings or behavior.

TRIGGER MECHANISM—A stimulus that acts as a psychological trigger, suddenly releasing other unrelated responses.

UNCONSCIOUS—That function of the mind that operates completely beyond the levels of awareness.

VENTING—Providing an escape for the release of pressure or suppressed feelings.

VULNERABLE—Open to attack or possible damage; not defensive.

EPITAPH

These precious words can only say
you loved me well and are ever loved by me.
I know we will join again.

About

the

Author

Wallace Sife, Ph.D., has long been in the private practice of psychotherapy, specializing in reading disorders, biofeedback and behavior modification. He has also trained and counseled in human bereavement. Since the untimely death of his beloved miniature Dachshund, Edel Meister, Dr. Sife has made a major change in the direction of his life, as well as his career. Now he works extensively, in private and group sessions, with bereaved people who are just learning that there is professional help available for them and their special grief.

Dr. Sife has lectured extensively and given seminars on pet bereavement and euthanasia. He participates in local support groups, and he took part in the filming of a TV veterinary series for PBS that dealt with pet bereavement and euthanasia. He helped plan some of the Pace University Annual Pets and People Conferences, and he is preparing future seminars in pet bereavement.

In addition to several other professional and personal affiliations, Dr. Sife has been a member of the Delta Society, American Psychological Association, Biofeedback Society of America and the Association for Thanatology; he is the founder and current president of the

Association for Pet Loss and Bereavement, organized with the enthusiastic participation of several of his pet bereavement patients and colleagues. He is an active member of the Dachshund Association of Long Island, and has been a successful breeder-owner-handler of miniature Dachshunds. Dr. Sife has also counseled on problem behavior in dogs. His section on comments, advice and responses to letters from members appeared as a regular feature in the bimonthly publication of the original Owner Handlers Association. He is also an acclaimed poet, and his book, *Modern Rubaiyat*, contains several quatrains on the death of beloved animals.

This volume on pet bereavement is lovingly dedicated to the memory of Dr. Sife's deceased dog, Edel Meister, CD, and to all other similarly loved pets throughout history. He now lives with his two adored miniature Dachshunds, Sheeba and her son, Pip.

INDEX